The Liberal Black Protestant Heterosexual Bourgeois Male

From W. E. B. Du Bois to Barack Obama

Paul C. Mocombe

UNIVERSITY PRESS OF AMERICA,® INC.
Lanham • Boulder • New York • Toronto • Plymouth, UK

Copyright © 2010 by
University Press of America,® Inc.
4501 Forbes Boulevard
Suite 200
Lanham, Maryland 20706
UPA Acquisitions Department (301) 459-3366

Estover Road
Plymouth PL6 7PY
United Kingdom

All rights reserved
Printed in the United States of America
British Library Cataloging in Publication Information Available

Library of Congress Control Number: 2009931595
ISBN: 978-0-7618-4801-1 (clothbound : alk. paper)
ISBN: 978-0-7618-4757-1 (paperback : alk. paper)
eISBN: 978-0-7618-4803-5

∞™ The paper used in this publication meets the minimum
requirements of American National Standard for Information
Sciences—Permanence of Paper for Printed Library Materials,
ANSI Z39.48—1992

Contents

Acknowledgments		v
1	Introduction to the Liberal Black Protestant Heterosexual Bourgeois Male	1
2	Heterosexual Protestant Bourgeois Liberalism	6
3	On the Interpretation of Du Bois's Double Consciousness	33
4	Double Consciousness and the Liberal Black Protestant Heterosexual Bourgeois Male Identity	53
5	Barack Obama and the Demystification of Black Double Consciousness	63
6	On the Interpretation of Obama's Double Consciousness	73
7	Black Consciousness Today and the *Liberal Black Protestant Heterosexual Bourgeois Male* Identity	87
8	*Fait Accompli*	98
References Cited		113
Index		127

Acknowledgments

The research for this work was conducted while the author was a Visiting Professor of Sociology at "the Great" Bethune-Cookman University. I am grateful to the faculty and staff (especially Mrs. Freddie Harris and Samantha Fils) for their intellectual stimulation and support. Drafting of the manuscript took place mainly in the Carl S. Swisher library on the Daytona Beach campus of the university, and at the new African American Research library in Fort Lauderdale, Florida. Members of the staff, Ethel Bush, Ballarie Ingram, Helen Morey, Judith Collier, and Tasha Youmans, at both centers provided library facilities and administrative services that made possible the completion of the writing within its appointed time.

My analysis and conclusions are a result of the mentoring of two great professors, the late Drs. Stanford M. Lyman and Teresa Brennan. To them I owe my intellectual and theoretical growth and framework. Lastly, I would like to thank my grandparents, Saul and Eugenia Mocombe, my spiritual mother Corliss Ann Russell, my wife, Tiara Mocombe, and my mother-in-law, Genetha Harris, who taught me why and how to love.

Chapter One

Introduction to the Liberal Black Protestant Heterosexual Bourgeois Male

On January 20th, 2009, Barack Obama was inaugurated as the 44th President of the United States of America in front of a crowd of over one million people on the National Mall of the capital in Washington, D.C. Running on a platform of change and optimism, Obama became the first African American elected to the highest office in the country. Interestingly enough, President Obama was elected not because his person represented physiological change because given the divisive nature of race relations in America many people never imagined there would be a black American elected to the presidency. Obama was elected on the fact that his person represents contradictory principles. He is the embodiment of both the ideals and social psychological identity, liberal bourgeois Protestantism, by which American society was constituted by the Founding Fathers of the nation, and the contradictory material practices of that very consciousness.

Obama's notion of change and optimism emanates from his embodiment of the liberal bourgeois Protestantism by which American society was constituted as a nation state, which stands in contradistinction to the anti-liberal and immoral historical experiences, racial slavery, represented by those who share his physiological racial type. Change in this essence is not a push away from notions of egalitarianism, class stratification, middle-class bourgeois ideology, and nationalism of the society, the so-called elements that facilitate The American Dream. Instead, the change and optimism Obama speaks of is a recommitment to these principles for all folks, over the (neo) conservatism of the Bush-era (2000–2008) and the socialism of the Cold-War era, amidst the dialectical material contradictions of liberal bourgeois Protestant cultural thought and practices as represented by the historical experiences and material conditions of people of color all over the world. In essence, Obama's notion of change has the audacity to promote hope (desire) for fruits which are

1

a result of a (re) commitment to the principles of the American nation state in spite of the contradictory practices Obama abhors reflected in the unequal material existence of people of color all over the world produced by the very principles of his Americanism.

The ambivalence is symbolically signified by Barack's physiology and social identity, liberal bourgeois Protestantism, which W.E.B. Du Bois (1903) brilliantly captures with his double consciousness construct. In fact, Barack's embodiment of American society's social psychological identity, and his subsequent success as an "other," legitimates the principles of the society in spite of the stratifications fostered by the very logic of the social system. It is the experience of being a liberal bourgeois Protestant "other" (simulacrum) that perpetually fosters the double consciousness by which both Du Bois and Obama constituted, and constitute, their identities.

Barack Obama is the embodiment of this social identity, *the liberal black Protestant heterosexual bourgeois male*, that contemporarily looks to serve as the bearer of ideological and linguistic domination for all people in America and world societies impacted by Western Protestant civilization in spite of contradictory material practices stemming from the identity which foster inequality, poverty, and ethnocentrism. The articulation of the discourse and discursive practices of Western Protestant liberal bourgeois civilization, and the contradictions therein for black folks as an "other" in that system are best represented in the double consciousness construct of W.E.B. Du Bois. Contemporarily, Obama is a paragon of and for the ambivalent struggle of Du Bois's construct. This work juxtaposes the ideals and practices of the two men in order to articulate and highlight the origins and nature of the discourse, discursive practice, and contradictions of this *soulless* (liberal bourgeois heterosexual male Protestantism) social psychological identity that has been seeking to institute its presence in the world since The Enlightenment despite its destructive material practice which threatens life and the concept of civilizations on earth.

In 1903, W.E.B. Du Bois in *The Souls of Black Folk* articulated what he thought to be the nature of black American consciousness, which has shaped contemporary understanding of African American life. According to Du Bois, building on the bourgeois ideology of nationalism to account for the constitutive identity of the black nation living side by side with white American society, the black American has a "double-consciousness," a "twoness," of being an American, and a Negro, "two warring ideals in one dark body, whose dogged strength alone keeps it from being torn asunder" (Du Bois, 1995 [1903]: 45). Through this conception, Du Bois attempted to constitute the social psychological identity of the black American nation and refute 19th century racial understanding of black life, which suggested that blacks were racially inferior to whites and had no culture or consciousness aside from that acquired through their contact with white people.

Du Bois's position, however, is rooted in a contradiction that stands against his American liberal bourgeois Protestant social identity by which he attempted to constitute the identity of the black nation. His "doubleness" identity of the black nation is grounded in the same racial science and ideology of biological determinism he attempted to refute. While the Americanness of black American life was a result of their sociocultural contact with whites, the cultural ideas and practices associated with their "Negro-ness" was grounded in their biologically determined racial type. Du Bois utilized the idea of race as a substance both biological and spiritual to inscribe black folk in a temporal community. A black nation defined by its "doubleness" and American bourgeois liberal Protestantism and Negroness within such liberal ideologies as individualism, reason, humanitarianism, enlightenment, egalitarianism, and classism.

Regardless of this contradiction by which Du Bois attempted to constitute black identity, bourgeois liberal Protestantism synthesized with communal "racial class" spiritualism. His construct nonetheless captured the discourse, discursive practice, and contradictions of the social identity he felt better explained the souls or consciousness of black folk, i.e. liberal bourgeois Protestantism amidst racial and class discrimination. Like Du Bois, Barack Obama is a progeny of this social identity, which has shown to be a soulless social identity, and has failed to resolve the class and racial dialectical contradictions it constitutes within liberal bourgeois racial Protestantism. The identity posits individualism, egalitarianism, enlightenment, and rationalism, while holding on to and reproducing racism, classism, authoritarianism, and inequality. An ambivalent struggle to reproduce the discursive practices of this social psychological identity amidst the classism, racism, and nationalism, was produced by that very consciousness Du Bois captures with his construct double consciousness. Du Bois wanted to reproduce his liberal bourgeois Protestantism while holding on to race, patriarchy, sexism, and classism, hence his double consciousness. Obama wants to reproduce his liberal bourgeois Protestantism by denying race, patriarchy, and sexism while holding on to classism, hence his double consciousness.

In order to better understand the problems with Du Bois's double consciousness as the ideological basis for black American consciousness in general, and Obama's in particular, this work attempts to outline a sociologically meaningful thesis on the development and nature of black American consciousness within the American liberal Protestant bourgeois capitalist social structure. I then (re) interpret W. E. B. Du Bois and Barack Obama's consciousness within the parameters of my sociological explanation and historical narrative in order to highlight the contradictory practices by which the identity is recursively organized and reproduced in its soulless aim capital accumulation.

The conclusions and practical implications drawn from this intellectual process are threefold. First, black American consciousness is not dual or bicultural nor is the black community a "real" community or nation, defined by its "doubleness" or dual ethnicity. Black American consciousness is instead multiple and diverse but dominated by the discursive practices of the liberal black Protestant heterosexual bourgeois males who for a long time served as the bearers of ideological and linguistic domination for the "black" community seeking equality of opportunity, distribution, and recognition for black folk.[1]

Second, the autobiographical construct of black double consciousness as highlighted by Du Bois should be understood more in relation to the purposive rationality, i.e. the imaginary "fictive ethnicity," or "class racism," (Etienne Balibar's terms) of the liberal heterosexual black (male) bourgeoisie who, following The Civil War, wanted equality of distribution and recognition with his white counterpart than as an externally valid construct representing the duality of black American social psychological identity. Du Bois, as a member of this social caste group, captures with the double consciousness construct their ambivalence toward American society, and the *desire* of his class to obtain the liberal promises of equality of opportunity, distribution, and recognition in American society against their *derision* for that same society because of its anti-liberal discriminatory practices against the black American due to their race and class positions in the society. Deconstructed from its reliance on nineteenth century racial science and ideology, double consciousness is actually a reference to Du Bois's ambivalence toward American society which was grounded in his class, status, and power position rather than an accurate representation of black American consciousness in the bicultural sense.

Finally, Du Bois of *The Souls* and Barack Obama represent an ideal type of and for this power elite of the American social structure who do not assume the liberal Protestant bourgeois social identity to resolve inherent contradictions that gave and gives rise to racism and classism but instead seeks to recursively organize and reproduce the praxis of the social identity to its purest form in order to be recognized by the white power elite of the society. Du Bois, theoretically, constructed the identity of the class for black (male) folk, and Obama, as I will demonstrate, is the embodiment of Du Bois' construct which is neither African nor enlightened but genuinely American and *soulless*. American liberal Protestant bourgeois capitalist society contradicts the very liberalism upon which its constitution was based and seeks to recursively reorganize and reproduce its practical consciousness for equality of opportunity and recognition amidst global oppression, exploitation, and devastation perpetuated by the dialectical logic of the very consciousness of liberal Protestant bourgeois society.

This work seeks to highlight the discourse, discursive practice, and contradictions of the social psychological identity as embodied by Du Bois and Obama. The work ostensibly is divided into two parts. The first half of the book deconstructs the origins of the social identity and the meaning behind Du Bois's double consciousness construct, which he initially utilized to represent the social psychological identity of black folk living in America. The second half of the book highlights Du Bois's articulation of the discursive practice of the discourse of the identity, which he was prevented from exercising because of white racial prejudice and discrimination, but which, as I demonstrate, Obama discursively seeks to practice contemporarily amidst reverse black racial prejudice and the class oppression of the society. In the end, the aim of the work is to highlight the contradictory ethos of the social psychological identity that has shaped black American life while paradoxically and simultaneously destroying it and all life on Earth.

NOTE

1. This is not the case today, as the black underclass is slowly becoming the bearers of ideological and linguistic domination in the larger society.

Chapter Two

Heterosexual Protestant Male Bourgeois Liberalism

The heterosexual Protestant male bourgeois liberalism of W.E.B. Du Bois and Barack Obama is a product of the ever-increasing purposive rationalization of a "mechanical" metaphysical worldview within the Protestant ethics and the spirit of capitalism which has been seeking to (paradoxically) immorally dominate the world and its plethora of civilizations through its metaphysical logic and Protestant Ethic since the Protestant Reformation of the sixteenth century. Those who have encountered this worldview either succumb to its metaphysical logic at the expense of their own, or perish in their attempts of resistance. The discourse and discursive practice of this worldview Max Weber brilliantly outlines in his work, *The Protestant Ethic and the Spirit of Capitalism*, to articulate the constitution of the individual personality that would come to constitute and attempt to dominate modern and world societies. Weber's structural logic better than any other serves as a theoretical framework for understanding the constitution of black American identity in Modernity.

The Protestant Ethic, as Max Weber (1958) points out, represents what was an understood set of values of rationality, hard work, economic gain as a sign of one's predestination, systematic use of time, and a strict asceticism with respect to worldly pleasures and goods. The values which he claims gave rise to the contemporary capitalist practices that constitute modern societies, and thus American capitalist society, within the global economic world-system, and the existing configuration of bureaucratic "Iron Cage" power relations within which, I argue, black practical consciousness developed.

The purposive-rational implementations by rich, white, Protestant, heterosexual men of these Protestant ideas and practices, rationality, hard work, economic gain as a sign of one's predestination, systematic use of time, and a strict asceticism with respect to worldly pleasures and goods, mediated and overdetermined by the concepts of race and nation, through the "ideological apparatuses" of governments, in other words, historicized social positions, based on reason, racial and national identity, and economic gain for its own sake through the accumulation of capital or profit in a "calling," i.e., class position, by which social actors or subjects constituted their "individual" identities, and were differentiated and subjugated (predestined or capitalists/ damned or laborers) in "modern" society.

This Weberian social psychological framework and understanding differs from both Marxist and non-Marxist structural interpretations of the constitution of modern society in that it begins with the cultural (ideal) conceptions that structured the social integrative practices that gave rise to modern western societies and the global economic world-system, while the Marxist, neo-Marxist, postcolonial, and liberal schools derive the terms of their analysis from the (material) social relations of production, or what amount to the same thing the systemic purposive-rational actions of the Protestant ethic (see Figure 2.1). The two viewpoints, systems and social integration, as my structural approach implies, are inextricably linked, however. Although philosophically we are able to think these two approaches, systems and social integration, apart as idealism and materialism, they are not necessarily entirely separable in reality.

Weber defines a capitalistic economic action

> as one which rests on the expectation of profit by the utilization of opportunities for exchange, that is on (formally) peaceful chances of profit. Acquisition by force (formally and actually) follows its own particular laws, and it is not expedient, however little one can forbid this, to place it in the same category with action which is, in the last analysis, oriented to profits from exchange. Where capitalist acquisition is rationally pursued, the corresponding action is adjusted to calculations in terms of capital. This means that the action is adapted to a systematic utilization of goods or personal services as means of acquisition in such a way that, at the close of a business period, the balance of the enterprise in money assets (or, in the case of a continuous enterprise, the periodically estimated money value of assets) exceeds the capital, i.e. [,] the estimated value of the material means of production used for acquisition in exchange (Weber, 1958: 17–18).

Although this relationship appears paradoxical since Protestant beliefs did not embrace the idea of economic gain for its own sake,

> Weber's argument is that the rational pursuit of the ultimate values of the ascetic Protestantism characteristic of sixteenth-and seventeenth-century Europe led people to engage in disciplined work; and that disciplined and rational organization of work as a duty is the characteristic feature of modern capitalism—its unique ethos or spirit (Marshall, 1998: 534).

Thus,

> The crucial link to Protestantism comes through the latter's notion of the calling of the faithful to fulfil their duty to God in the methodical conduct of their everyday lives. This theme is common to the beliefs of the Calvinist and neoCalvinist churches of the Reformation. Predestination is also an important belief, but since humans cannot know who is saved (elect) and who is damned, this creates a deep inner loneliness in the believer. In order therefore to create assurance of salvation, which is itself a sure sign (or proof) of election, diligence in one's calling (hard work, systematic use of time, and a strict asceticism with respect to worldly pleasures and goods) is highly recommended—so-called 'this-worldly asceticism'. In general terms, however, the most important contribution of Protestantism to capitalism was the spirit of rationalization that it encouraged. The relationship between the two is deemed by Weber to be one of elective affinity (Marshall, 1998: 535).

The affinity between the Protestantism of a sect and their purposive-rational actions, as I understand Weber to be saying, gave rise to the *economic* organization of modern society, systems integration, as the social psychological practices and ego-ideals (rationally calculating individuals attempting to prove their predestination reflected in their economic gains) of a form of Protestantism, social integration, were rationally and purposively incorporated into the physical world through the bureaucratic organization of the material resource framework around the state and economy in order to direct and constitute the identity and practices of social actors and societies. In some instances, bureaucratic means or structural practices (purposive-formal-rational action to organize the lived world) were established around already existing material elements which were re-conceptualized by the sect of rich, white, Protestant, men to foster a society based on wealth, economic gain or capital accumulation as a sign of their salvation in the eyes of God and others.

As these men and their ethos encountered social problems in their attempt to reconfigure or reconstitute sixteenth and seventeenth century European feudal governments along the lines of their Protestantism, they became a discriminated against "other" (Puritans, Pilgrims, Calvinists, Lutherans, etc.) minority in the Feudal (catholic) social structure of Europe of the middle ages. Subsequently, these newly created "others" left Europe and reformulated society, in the form of the American social structure by recursively organizing and reproducing their "other" form of being-in-the-world, i.e. Protestantism and the spirit of capitalism. The rules of conduct in the new American society were formulated to facilitate the relational logic, ends (substantive rationality), of their form of Protestantism, individualism, humanitarianism, rationalism, economic gain, or loss, as a sign of one's election or "damned-ness" in a particular "calling," which "embedded" social or cultural relations in what became the modern American political-economic system. With this sociohistorical conversion, within the Westphalian nation-state system, of Western society in general and American society in particular, from a catholic feudal social order to a Protestant capitalist social order through the purposive-rationality of rich, white, heterosexual Protestant men, the Protestant ethic became an allowed religion of the society, and thus the "metaphysical" ideas of the Protestant Church became joined with the power and discursive practices of the American Protestant nation-state government. This "invisible" marriage of church and state led to the formation of the "visible" universal ideals (liberalism, democracy, individualism, bourgeois classism, and nationalism) of the American nation-state under God, and over time caused the American nation-state/government to refine its doctrine and develop its structure in a way that best served its purposive-rational end, economic gain as a sign of the country and its citizens' salvation and predestination, within the emerging global (colonial) economic world-system.

In materialist terms, the endless accumulation of economic gain, capital, or profit by rich white Protestant men became "the defining characteristic and *raison d' être* of this [social] system," which over time pushed "towards the commodification of everything, the absolute increase of world production, and a complex and sophisticated social division of labor based on class" or the amount of capital (economic gain) one had accumulated (Balibar and Wallerstein, 1991: 107). As Jürgen Habermas concludes of this process by which the integrative substantive-rationality of a form of Protestantism, "the spirit of capitalism," came to dominate modern times by the systemic purposive-rational action of its power agents:

. . . economic production is organized in a capitalist manner, with rationally calculating entrepreneurs [(the predestined prosper)]; public administration is organized in a bureaucratic manner, with juristically trained, specialized officials — that is, they are organized in the form of private enterprises and public bureaucracies. The relevant means for carrying out their tasks are concentrated in the hands of owners and leaders; membership in these organizations is made independent of ascriptive properties [(today, maybe, but not the case for this type of society's early formation)]. By these means, organizations gain a high degree of internal flexibility and external autonomy. In virtue of their efficiency, the organizational forms of the capitalist economy and the modern state administration establish themselves in other action systems to such an extent that modern societies fit the picture of "a society of organizations," even from the standpoint of lay members (Habermas, 1987 [1981]: 306).

In this understanding of the origins and organizational basis of modernity and its paragon modern American capitalist society, where "the cultural struggle for distinction is intricately connected to the economic distribution of material goods, which it both legitimates and reproduces" (Gartman, 2002: 257), Weber's explanation, as Jürgen Habermas points out,

> . . . refers in the first instance not to the establishment of the labor markets that turned abstract labor power into an expense in business calculations, but to the "spirit of capitalism," that is, to the mentality characteristic of the purposive-rational economic action of the early capitalist entrepreneurs. Whereas Marx took the mode of production to be the phenomenon in need of explanation, and investigated capital accumulation as the new mechanism of system integration, Weber's view of the problem turns the investigation in another direction. For him the explanans is the conversion of the economy and state administration over to purposive-rational action orientations; the changes fall in the domain of forms of social integration. At the same time, this new form of social integration made it possible to institutionalize the money mechanism, and thereby new mechanisms of system integration (Habermas, 1987 [1981]: 313).

These two analytic levels, systems and social integration, are not separate if the understanding of the constitution of modernity is understood through my structural and organizational logic. The argument from this structural position is that the "predestined" white Protestant entrepreneurial males, a once marginalized group in pre-modern or feudal (catholic) Europe, by re-conceptualizing and maintaining the control of the then feudal market and state, reified their Protestant "practical consciousness." This Protestant metaphysical cultural value they rationalized with reality and existence as such, in institutions, the capitalist global market economy and bourgeois state, operating "through materialized metaphors beyond logical or empirical proof, on ungroundable premises, on nonobservable substances" (Friedland, 2002: 384), in order to mechanically and systemically constitute the identity and direct the agential moments or purposive-rationality of all social actors of the world for the sole purpose of accumulating economic gain (Marx's "capital accumulation") as a sign of their election or progress in the world.[1]

The organization of work for economic gain or profit in modern society was mechanically constituted as white Protestant males believing themselves to be "predestined" came as a social class to militarily dominate and control the ontological security of the world and its people of color, who they interpellated as the irrational damned or laborers working in order to (re) produce economic gain for those (predestined) who owned the means and modes of work or production. To put the matter simply, the logic here is that "the spirit of capitalism," which is characteristic of modernity in general and American society in particular, is the socioreligious discursive practice or purposive rationality of a form of cultural Protestantism that gave rise to the class identity of social actors, who became differentiated by their social behavioral (methodical) relation to the means and mode of work in modern societies. The

Heterosexual Protestant Bourgeois Liberalism 11

metaphysics of the Protestant Ethic, in other words, structured the physical world wherein individual social relations and actions were constituted and (re) produced (see Figure 2.1).

It should also be mentioned that modern societies in the global economic world-system, as all became interpellated as owners and workers, itself became a dialectical totality that underwent reproduction and transformation based on internal contradictions and class differentiation based upon capital accumulation motivated by the desire to acquire capital or economic gain for its own sake in the purposive-rationality of the Protestant Ethic (Balibar and Wallerstein, 1991; Smith, 1996). In fact, the modern political and economic ideologies of liberalism, conservatism, and radicalism are grounded in, and can be deduced from, the dialectical metaphysics of "the Protestant Ethic and the spirit of capitalism": radicalism representing a revolutionary response against the ideals and practices of liberal bourgeois heterosexual white male Protestantism that included bourgeois technical rationality, individualism, class inequality, racialism, and heterosexism; conservatism, representing strict commitment to its ideologies of individualism, class inequality, heterosexism, religiosity, and

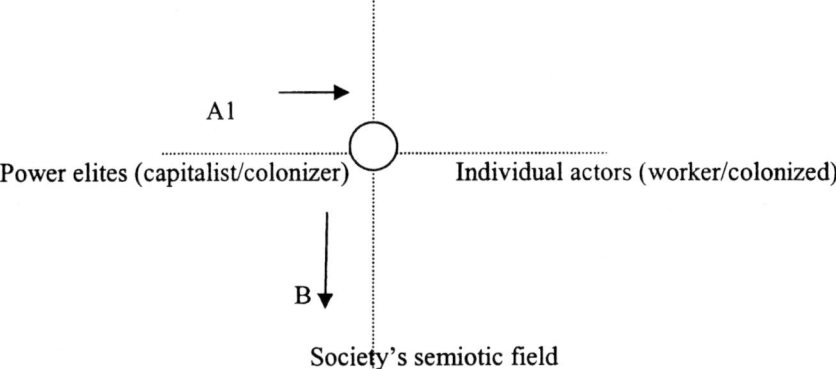

Figure 2.1. Diagram representing the structure of bourgeois culture. Capitalist interpretations (Marxist, Postmodernist, World-system, and dependency theories) view the synchronic axis (horizontal line) as resulting from the practices of the diachronic axis (the vertical line). The economic subjugation running along line A1 derives from the abstract laws (neoliberal policies) of institutional regulators (movement of line B), which rigidifies, i.e. reify, into the horizontal axis and is exported throughout the global (globalization).

My interpretation, in keeping with the structural logic of Max Weber (1958 [1905]), posits that the synchronic axis (Protestantism) gives rise to the diachronic (historical) practice—vertical axis—, capitalism, and globalization represents the means of localizing or structuring the global setting within the structure, or if you would, discourse of Protestantism, through capitalist practices, whether development (replication) models or market ones.

racialism; and liberalism was deduced from the Christian (Protestant) ethic of individual humanism, rationalism, anti-dogmatism, classism, and the liberal democratic capitalist state's ability to foster that ethic.

It is not the position here, however, that the "class racism" (Étienne Balibar's term) that would come to characterize the "white" American Protestant liberal bourgeois social order and black identity or practical consciousness is to be deduced solely from this systemic purposive-rationality of capitalist relations of production with its emphasis on global labor and capital accumulation grounded in the integrative metaphysics of the Protestant Ethic. As Etienne Balibar observes, "[mo]netary circulation and the exploitation of wage labour do not logically entail a single determinate form of state. Moreover, the realization space which is implied by accumulation—the world capitalist market—has within it an intrinsic tendency to transcend any [racial and] national limitations that might be instituted by determinate fractions of social capital or imposed by 'extra-economic' means" (Balibar, 1991: 89). Instead, the racial/national formation of the American state, it seems, has its development in the structure of its own concrete cultural historical development and form as opposed to a "bourgeois project," which is a historical myth "taken over by Marxism from liberal philosophies of history" (Balibar, 1991: 89). It is not enough to view the constitution of the American state through a materialist interpretation that only emphasizes the systemic economic purposive-rationality of those who would become the power elites (capitalists) of the social structure. This position neglects the overall integrative substantive-rationality (ideals) that grounded the purposive-rational actions of white Protestant heterosexual men to start with and offers a reductionist (class) view of the constitution of American society, modernity, and the global economic world system. The materialist argument overlooks the dialectical relationship between the integrative ideals and the systemic behaviors and stratifications which it fostered, class being just one of many.

We might overcome this liberal and Marxist one-sided materialist class view of the constitution of modernity in general and American society in particular through my structural perspective, which sees the modern constitution of society and the global economic world system through the power relations as highlighted by Weber's social psychological understanding of the constitution of modernity within a specific historical social formation, the American nation state, which would, after nationalizing and ethnicizing its population to resolve an internal contradiction in their Protestant ethic (slavery in the face of Christian brotherhood or human equality), come to constitute and direct the world capitalist market in order to accumulate profits or economic gain by modifying other social formations within the global economic world-system through the prism of its own local social formation, the racialization and nationalization of the protestant ethic and the spirit of capitalism.[2] It is within this Weberian social and systemic integrative structural logic that the constitution of black American identity or practical consciousness must be understood.

THE HISTORICAL CONSTITUTION OF AFRICANNESS IN THE AMERICAN RACIAL-CAPITALIST SOCIAL FORMATION

The distinct constitution of the American racial-capitalist social formation within the purposive-rationality of a capitalist world economy highlights the substantive and purposive-rational action of rich, white, Protestant heterosexual men. The formation becomes obscured if the focus is solely and simply on its systemic purposive rationality, i.e., the determinism of the global division of labor in the logic of capital accumulation as posited by most Marxists, or the notion of "primitive accumulation" posited by classic liberal thinkers. In both cases, the class basis of the arguments fails to account for and underplays the status roles of race, gender, and sexuality in the constitution of the American racial gendered capitalist social formation.

Just the same, the contemporary "communicative action" liberal discourse of Jürgen Habermas posits the political economy of the state as the product of the "communicative action" amongst the various status and party groups of the "public sphere" and obscures the purposive-rational action of rich, white, Protestant men, which in turn distorts the agential initiative of blacks in the society. Habermas's "communicative action" postulates the variability of social practices only in theory. A normatively "utopic" communicative paradise distorts the social conflict that arises between groups whose different province of meaning and action differs from those who absorb the purposive-rationality of the social structure as communicative discourse. Habermas underplays, and at times overlooks, the power relations (marginalization or segregation), in other words, by which the initial white "other" Protestant agents of "the spirit of capitalism" constituted the "public sphere" of their solidarity as a cultural system (Fraser, 1997).

The formation of the American nation state or social system in particular and modernity in general was not simply done "organically" through communicative purposive-rational action amongst the "predestined" white power agents of the society but "mechanically" as Weber's "iron cage" thesis implies.[3] White Protestant male social actors did not constitute modernity in general or American society in particular as a systemic framework or totality arrived at through mutually agreed upon sanctioned rational rules of conduct.

To the contrary, the discourse of modernity and American society resulted from the socioreligious substantive cultural values and practices of rich, white, heterosexual, Protestant men which were bureaucratically used to marginalize and discriminate against different provinces of meaning and behavior for their sole purposive-rationale of economic gain for its own sake or capital accumulation, which in the eighteenth century world colonial system psychologically had to be justified within the context of slavery (an institutional form for labor and capital accumulation), industrial development, gender and racial discrimination, and heterosexism.

It is within this mechanical constitution of modernity and American society, as opposed to Habermas' "utopic" normative model or the determinism of the division of labor, the dominant social form black American consciousness would take as constituted and directed by the black Protestant heterosexual male bourgeoisie (beginning with Du Bois) within the two antinomic poles, class and race, of a permanent dialectic, which is at the heart of modern liberal black American male representations of white American Protestant history.[4]

From this claim that the discourse of the Protestant Ethic within the discriminatory affects of industrial and agricultural development (organization of work), class, gender, and race, as opposed to Habermas's rational communicative discourse, Marx's "find," i.e., "the capitalist mode of production is constituted by 'finding already there' (*vorfinden*) the elements which its structure combines[,]"[5] or the bourgeois ideology of "so-called primitive accumulation," set the social structural conditions (in the form of the American social structure or society)—[6] which were in turn recursively organized and reproduced by social actors in material practice—black American "practical-consciousness" arose.[7] These "racial class" heterosexual gendered Protestant values, "enframed" by the global colonial economy, as they were institutionalized and recursively organized in the laws (US Constitution) and other ideological institutions or apparatuses such as the family, schools, and Protestant churches of American society, to regulate social practices for the systemic accumulation of capital or economic gain for its own sake in agricultural and industrial production, in other words, would have a long-term effect on the ways non-Protestant English and eventually non-European groups were interpellated, viewed, and dealt with and how they would come to interpellate, view, and deal with themselves in their relation to the means of producing capital or economic gain for its own sake in a colonial capitalist world system that underdeveloped Africa and other places of color while simultaneously, industrially, developing Europe and America (Hudson and Coukos, 2005; Cohen, 2002; Jones, 1971).[8]

Africans (an estimated 430,000 imported to North America during the whole period of the Atlantic Slave trade)[9] were like Native Americans and many poor whites had "other" forms of orientation in the world distinct from the Protestant form of the American social structure and its agents. The Africans encountered or were brought (1619–1808) into this once marginalized Protestant worldview as marginalized forced laborers and indentured servants in order to satisfy the idea of "economic gain" in agricultural production expropriated from the "damned" for the benefit of the industrially developed "predestined" in urban centers that the new Protestant—global economic—order ("slave-based plantation" agricultural capitalism)[10] proffered. In this ideologically economic driven new symbolic colonial world where the peoples of color of the world were commodified as agricultural workers to sustain the white industrial labor force of Europe and America, however, individual property rights were reconceptualized and elevated to a position sanctioned by divine authority and considered superior to all other rights, including the human rights and life of indigenous peoples, bonded laborers, and those who would eventually be bought as slaves (Smedley, 1999: 53; McMichael, 2008: 21). Thus, the institutional regulators (rich, white, Protestant, male landowners), given the need to maintain and reproduce the then bifurcated agriculturally/industrially based economic stratified order of things among those "others" who did not subscribe to it in order to sustain and maintain the labor force of white industrial workers, rationalized the labor requirements within what was already understood, the purposive-rationality of the Protestant Ethic and the spirit of capitalism. By the time America became a nation-state in the late eighteenth-century this stratification had already been established through the commodification of the African. In the bifurcated colonial order of bureaucratic social structural relations of white Protestantism and capitalism, Africans became the structurally differentiated undeveloped perpetual "black," non-Protestant, damned agricultural worker (commodity) who worked (as their property) *freely* for the industrially developed predestined white Protestants in order to maximize the rate of profit or economic gain in the colonial global economic system of the seventeenth, eighteenth, and nineteenth centuries.[11]

As the black radical nationalist thinker Maulana Karenga (1993) observed, several material factors made the enslavement of Africans for the increase of the rate of profit or economic gain in agricultural production to sustain the industrial labor force of Europe and America more feasible and permanent than that of other marginalized "damned" groups such as Native Americans and poor white indentured-servants:

> The first factor was Africa's closeness to the Caribbean where plantations were set up early and where Africans were "seasoned," i.e., made manageable, and then re-exported. Secondly, Africans already had experience in large-scale agriculture with their own fields and European plantations in Africa, unlike the

Native Americans who mainly hunted and gathered their food. Thirdly, Africans had relative immunity to European diseases due to long-term contact, whereas the Native Americans did not and were decimated at first by this.

Fourthly, the practicality of African enslavement rested in their low escape possibilities as opposed to Native Americans and whites due to unfamiliarity with the land, high social visibility and lack of a nearby home base. Fifthly, there were no major political repercussions for the enslavement of Africans, unlike the Native Americans who had people here to retaliate and the whites whose enslavement would challenge the tenets of Christianity and the age of enlightenment and reason on which Europe prided itself.

Finally, the basis of the American system of enslavement was in its justifiability in European racist thought. Although the enslavement of Africans was based in economic reasons, it also rested in racism as an ideology.... Racism as an ideology became a justification and encouragement for African enslavement (Karenga, 1993: 121–122).

These factors, however, were not perceived or conceived from a transcendental vantage point as Karenga's scientized material perspective implied. But their conjunctures were reasoned within what was already understood by those rich, white, Protestant, men in power positions in the society.[12] Their rationalization through the prism of their Protestant ideology or substantive-rationality would come to explain the social organization of the society and the structural framework by which African American practical consciousness was constituted.

The ever-increasing rationalization of the Protestant Ethic by rich, white, Protestant men progressively elaborated and expanded on themes of Christian brotherhood, human rights, and the elevation of the good of the many over the privileges of the few, which were recursively organized and reproduced through the "secular" practice or purposive-rationality of bourgeois racial, gender, and patriarchal capitalism that would come to constitute American society. The ideas of predestination through economic gain (as a sign of one's election or progress) justified the privileging of the good of the many (who were predestined to succeed—success being reflected in their economic gains or rate of profit) to have dominion over those who were not predestined and who were based on the structural (relational) logic of the former, undeveloped, backward, and damned. Those Protestants and non-Protestants, who were not predestined, like their predestined counterparts, were uncertain of their plight. They had to work hard in a particular calling for economic gain "as a sign." The enslaved, "damned" Africans, given their physical and behavioral differences, were rationalized in relation to the symbolic signifiers of white Protestantism. Interpellated in the White Protestant new world order, the Africans were not quite human to the white Protestants given the differences in African pigmentation, irrationalism, promiscuity, barbarity, carelessness, etc., and were therefore made to work for the whites. Class, and status position, and one's predestination were reflected in the rate of profit or economic gain obtained from the production of the "damned" and racial typology reinforced the belief in predestination.

Rich, Protestant, white, male factory and land owners (the power elites of the society), the "enlightened" and "progressive" predestined, institutionalized or rationalized their biblical, cultural, and entrepreneurial values into laws and practices, slave codes, miscegenation laws, systematic labor, capitalism, the individualism of civil rights and liberties, patriarchal family, and republicanism. Their values were embedded in pacts, agreements, the US and state constitutions and came to bureaucratically structure the political economy of the material resource framework within which the society became ensconced. At the same time structural or relational "blackness" and economic "class" developed as social categories (among others) for identity construction. More than anything else, this process of class and "racial"/ national differentiation, counterposed as it was by equalization between predestined rich, white, Protestant, men, was responsible for the dialectical totality that gave rise to the black practical consciousness that would come to constitute and dominate modern American society embodied in heterosexual black male bourgeois liberalism.

In terms of Habermas's theoretical communicative paradigm, the Protestant ideology and capitalist practices of society, institutionalized as laws and practices, are seen as the product of the "communicative action" of the varying groups (women, blacks, Jews, etc.) already existing within the society. My position, in keeping with the power relations highlighted by Marx's "ideological superstructure" and Weber's "Iron Cage" thesis, is the purposive-rationality of these laws and practices were utilized in the social institutions ("ideological apparatuses") of family, church, schools, organization of work (indentured servitude and slavery initially, consumerism and wage-labor, presently), etc., to condition or socialize (integrate) the masses—the constituting unit of the social structure—for the sole purpose of work or the reproduction of the American social relations of production, i.e. agricultural production in the South and industry in North. The acceptance and embodiment of these laws and practices gave the masses and the power elites or institutional regulators their practical consciousness or purposive-rationality, while all other forms of social action, arrived at through the deferment of meaning in ego-centered communicative action, and the structurally differentiated were marginalized and discriminated against as unequal and "other" by rich, white, Protestant, heterosexual men.

The Africans, ninety percent of whom could not read, were introduced (in 1619) as a marginalized unit of the structure and "seasoned" in the Protestant doctrines through slave codes, the Protestant churches (initially by white ministers, later on by native-born slaves), slavery, individual civil rights and liberties, etc. Unlike literate non-Protestant and Protestant whites who could work hard and eventually—if predestined—become masters or what amounted to the same thing institutional regulators, the structurally differentiated group of Africans had to accept their prescribed lowly conditions (slavery) given the fact that their physical difference and perpetual "otherness," in relation to white bourgeois (patriarchal) Protestantism, did not allow for their predestination or equality.

The relationship of Africans with the white, heterosexual, Protestant, power elites, therefore, operated along a master/slave relationship where the rich, white, Protestant males (masters) worked and re-worked the ideas and practices of the Protestant Ethic on the one hand and on the other their terms and representations for the Africans' forms (soul-less, blacks, savages and barbarous, less intelligent and human than their white counterparts, ungodly, promiscuous, undeveloped, etc.) of being in the world. The rich, white, Protestant, heterosexual males used the African representations to delimit their own form (godly, pious, urban, obedient, pure, civilized, diligent, intelligent, industrial, etc.) of being in the world and reproduced the colonial social relations of production through slavery and industrialism.

The Africans initially transported into this global "mechanical solidarity" in the seventeenth and early part of the eighteenth centuries were different and heterogeneous "others" with distinct practical consciousnesses. As a dominated deployable unit of the white Protestant economic social relations of American society they became a homogeneous group, blacks (later differentially stratified along class lines and their adaptive responses to enslavement) prepared for one facet of life in the American social structure, "systematic [agricultural slave] labor" (Blassingame, 1972: 3), conditioned by the obedient work ethic of Protestantism, which was juxtaposed against the industrial urban work of whites.

Africans came from all over Africa[13] and embodied different structurally determined subjective forms of being-in-the-world which ranged from rigid patriarchy and traditional Islamic practices to matrilineal polygamous tribalism. By the nineteenth-century (1808), which marks the discontinuation of the African slave trade to the United States, these "other" forms of being-in-the-world were discriminated against and marginalized within the American social structure. Native-born classified blacks, "the best of the house servants, mulattoes, artisans, and the educated free Negro from the North," due to their freedom and privileges, served as a reference group for the larger black community. They accepted, embodied, and recursively organized and reproduced the Protestant socioreligious cultural work ethos of the society in their material practices and purposive-rationality. Black identity or practical consciousness for them became, in keeping with the ethos of their white counterparts, synonmous with Protestantism, development, education, freedom, equality, wage-labor, and monogamous patriarchal family.

Given this response amongst the more free and powerful majority of the descendants of African slaves, who were barred from organizing and reproducing their African institutions within the material resource framework of the American Protestant bifurcated social and economic order, it is in terms of the structural variables (class and status, given the economic basis for the social relations of the society) of the Protestant American society, not other factors, that black consciousness in America became, can be, and has been assessed and determined. Other forms of practical consciousness amongst blacks within American society were defined and relationally delimited as "other" by these blacks, the "best" of the house servants, mulattoes, artisans, and the educated free Negro from the North, who, when they became institutional regulators within the American social structure, delimited or represented the "proper" and "pure" way of being-in-the-world for all blacks in terms of Protestant liberal heterosexual bourgeois practical consciousness, interests, ideals, habitus, etc.

Thus, "after the end of the [(slave)] trade in America in the latter half of the eighteenth and early part of the nineteenth centuries [Africanisms] importance as an explanation of slave personality declines: only about 400,000 native-born Africans had been brought to the United States before 1807 [(the slave trade, as sanctioned by the US Constitution, legally ended in 1808)]. Since an overwhelming percentage of nineteenth-century Southern slaves were native Americans" (Blassingame, 1972: 39), they, about 3,953,760 of the black population at the outbreak of the Civil War, had to construct their identity or consciousness as a deployable unit of the American social structure in relation to and led by "the best of the house servants, who were freed by their masters, [and] the educated free Negro from the North" who together numbered about 500, 000, twelve percent of the total black population, "at the outbreak of the Civil War"[14] (See Table 2.1)

It was not "in the process of acculturation the slaves made European forms serve African functions" (Blassingame, 1972: 17) as many representatives of the adaptive-vitality school contend (Allen, 2001; Asante, 1988, 1990; Billingsley, 1968, 1970, 1993; Blassingame, 1972; Early, 1993; Gilroy, 1993; Gutman, 1976; Herskovits, 1958 [1941]; Holloway, 1990a; Karenga, 1993; Levine, 1977; Lewis, 1993; Lincoln and Mamiya, 1990; Nobles, 1987; Staples, 1978; Stack, 1974; West and Gates, 1997; West, 1993). On the contrary, the majority of slaves had to relationally define and choose, for their ontological security within the American social structure, between the European forms prescribed by power (whites and the best of the house servants, mulattoes,

Table 2.1. Growth of the Slave and Free Negro Population in the United States 1790–1860

| | NEGRO POPULATION | | | |
| | | Free | | |
CENSUS YEAR	Total	Number	Per Cent	Slave
1860	4,441,830	488,070	11	3,953,760
1850	3,638,808	134,495	11.9	3,204,313
1840	2,873,648	386,293	13.4	2,487,355
1830	2,328,642	319,599	13.7	2,009,043
1820	1,771,656	233,634	13.2	1,538,022
1810	1,377,808	186,446	13.5	1,191,362
1800	1,002,037	108,435	10.8	893,602
1790	757,181	59,557	7.9	697,624

Note. Adapted From *The American Negro: His History and Literature* (p. 5), by E. Franklin Frazier, 1968, New York: Arno Press and The New York Times. Copyright 1968 by Arno Press, Inc.

artisans, and the educated free Negro from the North) or the continual practice of their ontologically insecure "other" (African) forms of being-in-the-world or any "other" fully visible, albeit discriminated against, "alternatives," which delimited the social structure.

This does not mean that nothing of Africa survived slavery because of the African's need to forsake African forms in order to move from being "other" in American Protestant liberal bourgeois society. The suggestion is different alternative categorical boundaries existed in the African community, and it was the "practical consciousness" of "the best of the house servants, mulattoes, artisans, and the educated free Negro from the North" that, to a large extent rejected African forms in order to be recognized by their white masters. Rejection of African forms would come to represent and define black identity as these blacks became institutional regulators and the bearers of ideological and linguistic domination within the "class racism" of the dominant Protestant American society (Winant, 2001).

In terms of structural logic, in the development of American society within an emerging global economic colonial world-system, white, Protestant males developed a series of laws and judicial rulings, "enframed" (Heidegger's term) by the cultural metaphysical ideology of their protestant ethic, to define and represent the African (black cursed son of Ham, ungodly, licentious, emotional, undeveloped, irrational, uncivilized and barbaric, soul-less, etc.) situation in relation to whites (white, godly, pious, obedient, pure, civilized, diligent, rational, industrial, developed, etc.). Whites' morally justified (given the internal contradiction between slavery and Christian brotherhood, human rights, etc.) reproduced the integrative economic (Protestant) social relations of agricultural production (slavery) proffered by them as the predestined or power elites of the society to sustain their industrial developed base and bring about civilization to the black backward undeveloped "damned" African. As the historian Vincent D. Harding (1981) highlights,

> Beginning in Virginia at the end of the 1630s, laws establishing lifelong [(*durante vita*)] African slavery were instituted.[15] They were followed by laws prohibiting black-white intermarriage, laws against the ownership of property by Africans, laws denying blacks all basic political rights (limited as they were among whites at the time). In addition, there were laws against the education of Africans, laws against the assembling of Africans, laws against the ownership of weapons by Africans, laws perpetuating the slavery of their parents to African children, laws forbidding Africans to raise their hands against whites even in self-defense.
> Then, besides setting up legal barriers against the entry of black people as self-determining participants into the developing American society, the laws struck another cruel blow of a different kind: they outlawed many rituals connected with African religious practices [(which were deemed heathenistic, lewd, licentious, etc.)], including dancing and the use of the drums. In many places they also banned African languages. Thus they attempted to shut black people out from both cultures, to make them wholly dependent neuters.
> Finally, because the religious and legal systems were so closely intertwined, everywhere in the colonies a crucial legislative decision declared that the Africans' conversion to Christianity [(the Protestant type)] did not affect their enslavement. . . . Again, Virginia led the way: in 1667 its Assembly passed an act declaring that "the conferring of baptism doth not alter the condition of the person as to his bondage or freedome." Such laws freed many whites to do their Christian duty of evangelization and to reap the profit and the social standing of slave ownership at the same time (27).

Africans who began arriving on the North American mainland "over more than a century preceding the War of Independence" (Gutman, 1976: 328) did not initially subscribe to this racial, class, gendered, patriarchal ideological foundation. They resisted enslavement and its institutionalization through ship mutinies prior to their arrival to the "New World;" guerilla wars; rebellions, the New York City Revolt in 1712, the Stono, South Carolina revolt in 1739, Gabriel Prosser revolt in 1800, Denmark Vesey conspiracy in 1822, the Nat Turner revolt in 1831, etc.—over 250 revolts are recorded in the US; suicide and infanticide; flights; and sabotage, i.e., breaking tools and destroying crops, shamming illness or ignorance, taking property, spontaneous, and planned strikes, work slow-downs, self-mutilation, arson, attacks on whites and poisoning of slaveholders and their families (Karenga, 1993; Bennett, 1982; Harding, 1981; Blassingame, 1972; Gutman, 1976; Aptheker, 1964; Franklin and Moss, 2000). These efforts, however, proved to be counter productive to resisting subjugation, as they were incorporated by the white masters as evidence of the African's barbaric or savage disposition. The image of the African as unruly, rebellious, irrational, stupid, prone to thievery, destructive, sophomoric, licentious, were in turn used, relationally, to demonstrate to the slaves—during the "seasoning" process where the African learned Protestantism and its systematic work ethic—what was unacceptable behavior of a barbaric black slave without religion.

As the historian John Blassingame (1972) points out in *The Slave Community*, "white ministers taught the slaves that they did not deserve freedom, that it was God's will that they were enslaved, that the devil was creating those desires for liberty in their breasts, and that runaways would be expelled from the church. Then followed the slave beatitudes: blessed are the patient, blessed are the faithful, blessed are the cheerful, blessed are the submissive, blessed are the hardworking, and above all, blessed are the obedient" (Blassingame, 1972: 62–63).[16] During the "seasoning" process, where the newly arrived Africans were forcefully taught by slave masters, over-seers and native-born slaves the language, religion, and work ethic (purposive-rationality) of the Protestant American social structure. The majority of the early slaves, Stanley Elkins's (1959) Sambo, who worked intimately with their white masters, for their ontological security, incorporated these beliefs and practices, which they recursively organized and reproduced in their own material practices, and they became the structural terms of "good moral character, economic accumulation, temperance, industry, thrift, and learning," by which the larger slave community, which either maintained some element of their Africanisms in their material practices or developed a pathological-pathogenic form of the structural terms of the society given their relative isolation, was assessed (Elkins, 1959; Frazier, 1939, 1957; Stampp, 1956; Genovese, 1974).

With their very survival dependent upon following rules of sanctioned conduct, many Africans accepted and acculturated or accommodated to the institution of slavery and incorporated the Protestant ethos (its work ethic, family organization, "white standards of morality," godliness, obedience, rationalism, etc.) into their way of being-in-the-world or what amounted to the same thing the social structure (Elkins, 1959; Frazier, 1939, 1957; Stampp, 1956; Genovese, 1974). They and the dominant whites, as bearers of ideological and linguistic domination, used that Protestant socioreligious work ethos to assess and determine the proper rules of conduct for the larger slave community.[17]

Those who did not accommodate were for the most part killed or brutally tortured until they complied. As a deployable unit, black slaves of the social structure, the social organization of family and cultural life in the majority of the African slave quarters became based on the ethical rules of the Protestant Ethic against fully visible African ways of being-in-the-world, as demonstrated in the practices of newly arrived Africans or those who, through the constitution of alternative meanings and behaviors through ego-centered communicative discourse, either rejected the substantive and purposive-rationality of the American social structure or sought to exercise them in "a national position"[18] of their own. This latter group of blacks included maroone communities of runaway slaves who attempted to exercise their African agential moments in the new world order, and nationalist and conservative literate black leaders such as Booker T. Washington, David Walker, Gabriel Prosser, Denmark Vesey, Nat Turner, Martin Delany, Henry Highland Garnet, etc., who, although they embodied the Protestantism of the social structure, sought not integration, like the majority of their liberal bourgeois male counterparts, but separation and black nationalism (Meier, 1963, 1966; Stuckey, 1987).

Consequently, the agential moments of those blacks who failed to exercise the substantive and purposive-rationality of the society, or rejected it in order to exercise them in "a national position" of their own, were discriminated against and marginalized. Slave owners, white overseers, and native-born acculturated liberal blacks, "the best of the house servants, mulattoes, artisans, and the educated free Negro from the North," recursively organized and reproduced the purposive-rationality of the social structure, "the standard of good society," i.e., "temperance, industry, thrift, and learning," in their own material practices, for the sole purpose of integration in order to obtain equality of opportunity, distribution, and recognition in the society with their white counterparts (Meier and Rudwick, 1966 [1976]: 127).[19]

What developed from all this was a class-color-caste system, i.e. a "racial caste in class," superordinate industrial whites and subordinate agricultural blacks, perpetually subordinate, each dominated by the "predestined" class. Blacks in relation to whites, in other words, emerged in the social structure of the "spirit of colonial capitalism" as a caste (a racial class-in-itself as a result of "racial" structural differentiation) defined by their inherent fitness for slave labor to produce economic gain for their white masters, to a "caste in class" defined in relation to whites by those good obedient slaves (Stanley Elkins' Sambo, resulting from "class" structural differentiation), who embodied the Protestant work ethic of the society for the sole purpose of integration or proving their predestination and those who did not because of their lack of "class" or need for separation.

This racial class social system became "reinforced" by the sociopolitical, religious, economic "legal system" (slavery and Jim Crow segregation) in which the majority of the Africans followed the rules of conduct which were sanctioned by the master for the slave and himself (Drake, 1965: 3).[20] The majority of the slaves, given their "seasoning" in the American Protestant solidarity as a structurally differentiated racial class-in-itself, black slaves,[21] recursively organized and reproduced the rules of their masters, against the reproduced negative images (unruly, barbaric, savages, etc.) of themselves by these same masters. To demonstrate their "predestination," or a sense of self-worth, blacks acculturated European and Protestant practices within the social structure among themselves: jumping over the broomstick to legalize marriages, an old English tradition commonly used instead of church weddings, which were illegal for slaves; establishing traditional patriarchal nuclear families based on monogamy; establishing, as a result of segregation, Masonic lodges, churches, and mutual aid societies patterned after their white counterparts; demonstrating diligence in their work; instilling in their children a sense of Christian values;[22] black hymns; penning petitions for their liberation—the idea "that God granted temporal freedom, which man, without God's consent, had stolen away" (Blassingame,1972: 63),—based on reason and revelation as their white masters did against England; and a developing class distinction (also based on color, lighter blacks v, darker ones) between house, "mixed-bloods," Negroes and field slaves, the former, given their close ties to the slave owner and quasi-freedom, better off then the latter (Franklin, 1957; Karenga, 1993; Bennett, 1982; Harding, 1981; Blassingame, 1972; Gutman, 1976; Apteker, 1964; Franklin and Moss, 2000).[23]

This acculturation for survival in essence eventually turned African consciousness among a *few* blacks, "favored" slaves, house slaves, artisans, "mixed-bloods," free colored population, who together numbered about 500, 000 at the outbreak of the Civil War, into an American, black heterosexual liberal bourgeois Protestant type. A practical consciousness amongst many blacks defined (by black heterosexual men) by their struggle for freedom, to exercise the purposive-rationality of the social structure and obtain class and status "based upon possession of money, education, and family background as reflected in distinctive styles of behavior" (Drake, 1965: 3), against the claim of "their inherent fitness for slavery and backwardness" which delimited the social structure and barred them from achieving economic gain and recognition. This social psychological identity, represented most dynamically in the figure W.E.B. Du Bois, stood in contradistinction to black heterosexual male conservatism, black nationalism, the ethos of black folk culture, and the pathologies of the black underclass. In fact, heterosexual black male bourgeois Protestant liberalism would come to dominate as the dominant social psychological identity and player in the black quest for freedom, paradoxically, from the vagaries and contradictions of liberal bourgeois heterosexual white male Protestantism.

American society was founded on the rationales of rich, white, Protestant men, i.e. the predestined master capitalist class. As the laws (US and State Constitutions) they enacted and institutionalized, based on their biblical, cultural, and entrepreneurial practices, "sought to provide legal sanction to the economic, political, and cultural domination and definition of the black captives from Africa by the whites from Europe, many of those laws at the same time, as part of the same objective, aimed at building a new fundamentally false solidarity between the upper and lower classes of the white population" (Harding, 1981: 28). This racial ideology of white nationalism ("class racism") used to justify the differentiation accorded to blacks amidst the universalism and equalization of the Protestant ethic and the spirit of capitalism was entirely compatible with the economic individualism of the Protestant ethic, and expanded positions of power to include, eventually, all white males (as the Constitution referred to "all persons," Africans before the passage of the Fourteenth Amendment did not count as persons—they were three-fifths of a person) antagonistic to blacks and their concerns.[24]

Blacks, consequently, shared in this structure of signification in that they were a discriminated against homogenized minority, "damned" black slave agricultural workers, whose behaviors, as prescribed by the white majority through institutions, the black church, slaves laws or codes, etc., had to reflect that of good, Christian servants (Sambo), as opposed to the barbarity associated with their Africanness or any other alternative forms, black maroon communities, black nationalist groups, black homosexuals, feminists, etc., of being-in-the-world arrived through the deferment of meaning in ego-centered communicative action, lest their ontological security became threatened.

Be that as it may, it is not the case that as a structurally differentiated discriminated against and marginalized group, blacks "made common choices rooted in a cumulative slave experience" in which other alternative (adjustments to enslavement) black forms of being-in-the American social structure, were incorporated into a larger community or value system (Gutman, 1976: 103,155).

The slave community, whose total slave population was of the order of 4 million by 1860,[25] was heterogeneous (adaptation took many forms), relationally defined by the different adjustments to enslavement and oppression within the larger slave community, which by the end of the Civil War was defined and determined by the adjustments of those blacks, who, for their ontological security, incorporated the Protestant rules of conduct or cultural structure of the larger American community, and therefore were accorded better social positions in the American caste system.

This group of blacks, "the black bourgeoisie" (E. Franklin Frazier's terms), marginalized and discriminated against all other black adaptive responses which they deemed, or represented as, pathological-pathogenic in relation to their racialized liberal bourgeois Protestantism. They believed following bourgeois Protestant rules of conduct accorded them better equality of opportunity and recognition with their white counterparts (Frazier, 1939; 1957). Black Protestant male "practical consciousness," therefore, became defined within the two antinomic poles of race and class by its bourgeois liberalism and racial nationalism. They recursively organized and reproduced the Protestant Ethic in a racial nationalist position of their own in order to obtain equality of opportunity, distribution, and recognition for all blacks in the larger American society. This Du Boisian purposive-rationale was juxtaposed against the folk cultural ethos of the black underclass in the agricultural South, the bourgeois conservatism of Booker T. Washington, and the radical black nationalism of Henry Highland Garnett and Marcus Garvey who sought to recursively organize and reproduce the Protestant Ethic in a bourgeois separate and nationalist position.

The liberal black Protestant (male) heterosexual bourgeois practical consciousness over time did not only become the dominant discourse in American society in general, and black America in particular, but constantly had to (re) define itself in relation to the discursive practices of black feminists, gays, whites, black conservatives, black nationalists, and the black underclass. Herein lies the origin of Du Boisian double consciousness. The ambivalent estrangement of the liberal black bourgeoisie is the nature of their own "class racism" and Du Bois's double consciousness. The struggle and *desire* to define and prove black self worth by obtaining equality of opportunity and recognition through their hard work, temperance, education, is coupled with their *derision* for the discriminatory effects of the white Protestant bourgeois society. The racial and class marginalization they experience within the dominant white society due to their "other" (African) forms of orientation in the world as represented in the practical consciousness of black nationalists and the black poor, which they also discriminate and define themselves against, are used by their white counterparts to bar them from economic gain, equality, and recognition. Producing an ambivalence in the liberal black Protestant heterosexual bourgeois male, which Du Bois captures with his doubleness construct.

As Adolph Reed (1997) points out in his analysis of Du Bois's work *The Philadelphia Negro*, which gives an insight into Du Bois's view of the world: "[t]he strengths of Philadelphia's black community [(according to Du Bois)] are seen as those of its characteristics that most approximate the model of bourgeois [Protestant] convention; the weaknesses that Du Bois identifies are those characteristics that most flaunt the conventional model. Broadly speaking, this model emphasizes, among other things: (1) monogamous nuclear family organization; (2) temperance and orderliness as behavioral principles, including thrift and internalization of disciplined work habits; (3) favorable disposition toward formal education and training in the ways of urban civilization; and (4) legitimation of class hierarchy within the racial community" (1997: 28). Du Bois desired to be an American amidst America's marginalization of people who look like him because of their racial and economic class positions determined by the very Americanism Du Bois yearned for and ambivalently denounced, i.e. Du Boisian double consciousness.

So how is it that W.E.B. Du Bois and contemporary theorists intuit a double consciousness in the bicultural sense amongst a distinct people whose sole aim was to "attain self conscious manhood, to merge his double self into a better and truer self," when institutions associated with their original African way of being were outlawed and replaced with new ideological apparatuses, the nuclear family, church, education, capitalism, etc., relationally intended to foster a distinct way of life (the Protestant ethic and its practices, the Spirit of Capitalism) as led by "the best of the house servants, [and] the educated free Negro from the North"? Du Bois, Reed points out, could do so only by relying on the neo-Lamarckian biological determinist outlook as mediated by the bourgeois ideology of nationalism, which dominated late nineteenth and early twentieth century social thought. Du Bois, like his white contemporaries, utilized the idea of race as a substance both biological and spiritual (i.e., the "souls" of black folk) to inscribe black folk in a temporal community (black nation within a nation) defined by their "doubleness." Today, given the refutation of this biological and ideological perspective (Balibar and Wallerstein, 1991 [1988]), many scholars (of the adaptive-vitality school) continue to articulate Du Bois's position because of the cultural turn (which supplants race and nation) in analysis that concentrates on the physical body as the site for cultural meaning and signification irrespective of the practices the body exercises.

My structural understanding of the constitution of black American consciousness within the American liberal bourgeois Protestant solidarity dismisses both points without, however, dismissing Dr. Du Bois's double consciousness construct which has shaped contemporary understanding of black consciousness as revealed in the discourse and discursive practice of both Du Bois and President Barack Obama. Even though the majority of black Americans, as a result of their attempt to "attain self conscious manhood" within one dominant structure of signification, developed multiple and diverse practices dominated by one dominant consciousness, the purposive-rationality of the Protestant type and its practices, the spirit of capitalism, by which all other "alternative" black forms of being-in-the-world arrived at through the deferment of meaning in ego-centered communicative action were delimited and assessed, nevertheless, the ambivalence that arises amongst this dominant group, the heterosexual, black, Protestant, bourgeois male, who are discriminated against as they seek economic gain and recognition amidst racial and class differentiation in the society, engenders a feeling of "doubleness," desire and derision.

The ambivalence has no basis in a different epistemology and or ontology in the discriminated-against black, as traditional interpretations of Du Boisian double consciousness implies, but is a result of having their presence serve as the "other" delimiting term which relationally defines the structure they attempt to be within, in order to deny their purposive-rationale, economic gain for its own sake and recognition. Hence, the "doubleness" Du Bois, as a paragon of this racial class, intuits and autobiographically articulates in *The Souls of Black Folk* is the ideological articulation of the liberal black bourgeoisie's ambivalence about American society; their desire to achieve economic gain and recognition in the society, by exercising the agential moments of the society, and derision for that same society for its discriminatory practices which deny them the equality of opportunity, distribution, and recognition they seek for themselves and the black masses, who remain a permanent segregated underclass in the society because of the (racial class) discriminatory effects of the society stemming from the very consciousness the black Protestant male majority desire to exercise.[26]

The discourse and discursive practices of W.E.B. Du Bois and Barack Obama represent this ambivalence of the liberal black Protestant heterosexual bourgeois male. Obama's struggle is a twenty-first century parallel to Du Bois's own nineteenth-century struggles to be a liberal black Protestant heterosexual bourgeois male amidst the contradictory practices of their very consciousnesses. Whereas Du Bois articulates his struggle within an American intellectual atmosphere that emphasized racial worldviews, Obama's struggle takes place in an intellectual social atmosphere wherein his liberal black Protestant heterosexual bourgeois male identity is bounded more by his class position, which is neither African or African American but genuinely American and *soulless*, than his mix-raced background, which makes a potential patron for the plethora of black commodified racial worldviews seeking his patronage. Hence, whereas Du Bois's struggle was to be recognized as a liberal *black* Protestant heterosexual bourgeois male in spite of the fact that he was black, Obama's struggle is to be recognized as a liberal Protestant heterosexual bourgeois male against being black or a hyphenated-American.

NOTES

1. This is the process in socialization that Habermas refers to as "the colonization of the life-world".

2. This is what Etienne Balibar calls the "fictive ethnicity," "the community instituted by the nation-state" (Balibar and Wallerstein, 1991 [1988]: 96).

3. Weber's determinism is not an off-shoot of his idealism in *"The Protestant Ethic and the Spirit of Capitalism"*. On the contrary, the iron cage thesis becomes determinist because of Weber's observation that Protestant social actors reify their Protestant ideals through the bureaucratization of society.

4. I focus on race and class because it is my position that these two poles have not been analyzed adequately together. bell hooks does a masterful job in looking at the roles of sex and gender in the constitution of black identity.

5. Karl Marx quoted in Balibar, Étienne (1968 [1970]: 283). "Elements for a Theory of Transition," pp.273–308. In *Reading Capital*, Louis Althusser and Étienne Balibar. London: NLB.

6. It is this sort of Polanyian (cultural) understanding of social relations "embedded" in the economic system which guides my theoretical conception of the nature of the American ideological mechanical social structure. Although, in my view, it was the rationalization of Protestant ideals as capitalist practices that resulted in Anglican, Puritan, and other Englishmen (a discriminated against minority in the feudal social structure of The Middle Ages) recursively organizing and reproducing the culture to establish what would become the system/social integration we call the United States of America.

7. Stanley M. Elkins's *Slavery: A Problem in American Institutional and Intellectual Life* (1959) building on Frederick Jackson Turner's "frontier thesis" makes this capitalist argument. It is, however, my position that Elkins fails to account for the agency of the slaves within the American capitalist/paternalist social structure. See Herbert Gutman's *The Black Family in Slavery and Freedom, 1750–1925* (1976) for a critical critique of Elkins.

8. Jürgen Habermas sees this "colonization of the lifeworld" as a crisis; I see it as the basis of societal integration.

9. See Philip D. Curtin, *The Atlantic Slave Trade: A Census* (Madison, 1969), Pp.72–87.

10. See William Julius Wilson's *The Declining Significance of Race: Blacks and Changing American Institutions* (1978) for the economic and political dynamics involved in shaping Southern institutions.

11. Whether on large plantations or small ones, all enslaved Africans in interaction with whites developed their practical consciousness by warring against the ways of the slave master and what they said the slaves were based on the fully visible behavior of newly arrived Africans.

12. In my structural understanding, the origins of American slavery, and its relation to the ideology of racism, are social structural. Slavery in America was not an autonomous system which developed out "of the condition and status of seventeenth-century labor" (Elkins, 1968 [1972]), but, as Oscar and Mary F. Handlin imply (albeit for the Handlins their position was also in reference to economic conditions whereas I am taking their reference to encompass a structuring ontology that gives rise to institutions), slavery "emerged rather from the adjustment to American conditions of traditional European institutions" (Handlins, 1950 [1972]: 23), which gave rise to the necessary conditions for the ever-increasing need for cheaper labor-power, which was in-turn rationalized or justified within the order of things, i.e., the Protestant ethic and the spirit of capitalism.

This synthesizing position, in the debate among historians of slavery as to the origins of racism in the United States, sides with Winthrop Jordan (1962 [1972]) who sees "both slavery and prejudice as species of a general debasement of the Negro," which stemmed, as Carl Degler (1959 [1972]) points out, from a stratifying, and discriminatory worldview bent on oppressing and exploiting (since the aim was extracting the most value out of labor for economic gain) the means it deemed necessary to meet or live out its end or ontology, i.e., economic gain for its own sake. In my view, accordingly, it is not enough to look at the material conditions, but on the contrary the structuring ontology by which the material condition is structured or recursively organized and reproduced.

13. See Joseph E. Holloway, "The Origins of African-American Culture," in *Africanisms in American Culture* (1990). Bloomington and Indianapolis: Indiana university Press, Pp. 2.

14. See E. Franklin Frazier's *Black Bourgeoisie* (1957), Pp. 15.

15. Massachusetts, founded by the Pilgrims, a Protestant sect, became the first colony (1641) to pass any enslavement laws.

16. It is no surprise that the seven major historic black denominations—the African Methodist Episcopal (A.M.E.) Church; the African Methodist Episcopal Zion (A.M.E.Z.) Church; the Christian Methodist Episcopal (C.M.E.) Church; the National Baptist Convention, U.S.A., Incorporated (NBC); the National Baptist Convention of America, Unincorporated (NBCA); the Progressive National Baptist Convention (PNBC); and the Church of God in Christ (COGIC)—that account for more than 80 percent of black religious affiliation in the United States are of the Baptist, Methodist, and Pentecostal Protestant variety. These Protestant churches with their high emotionalism, fervor, enthusiasm, and excitement, their revivalism, their excesses of sinning and high-voltage confessing (Bell, 1960: 103), have provided—for an illiterate mass prevented for a long time, on account of their immorality, lasciviousness, and heathenism, from partaking in the "thisworldly" affairs of the Protestant American social structure, derived from the intellectualism of traditional Protestantism—the means for access, via what is required for "otherworldly" existence, into the "thisworldly" affairs of the social structure.

In other words, for blacks, the Christianity of Methodism and Baptism served as a means to the Protestant ethic and the spirit of capitalism, the structuring structure of the culture that is American society. The "Christianity that was spread among slaves during the First and Second Awakenings was an evangelical Christianity that stressed personal conversion through a deep regenerating experience, being born again. The spiritual journey began with an acknowledgement of personal sinfulness and unworthiness and ended in an emotional experience of salvation by God through the Holy Spirit. The rebirth meant a change, a fundamental reorientation in the approach to life" (Lincoln and Mamiya, 1990: 6)—becoming moral agents of the Protestant ethic in "this world" in order to have access to the "other world."

17. Some historians argue that the period prior to the cessation of the slave trade was more brutal and harsh than the period after the ban when slave masters relied almost completely on natural increase to reproduce the labor force. In my view, this distinction underestimates the degree to which the enslaved blacks' ontological security (the degree of brutality and oppressiveness) was attached to following plantation

rules of conduct. In essence, my position is whether benign or brutal the general intent of the institution of slavery, as an ideological institution, was to inhibit the general autonomy and determine the agential moments of blacks. Just like the general intent of the organization of work in contemporary times is to maintain the capitalist social relations of production and determine the agential moments of all wage laborers.

18. Martin Robinson Delany quoted in August Meier and Elliott Rudwick, *From Plantation to Ghetto* (New York, 1976), Pp. 151.

19. As August Meier and Elliott Rudwick (1966 [1976]) point out, this was the platform of the "Negro Convention Movement," which began in 1830 and met annually until the end of the century. A predominantly Northern phenomenon, "led and attended by the most distinguished leaders of the race—prominent ministers, physicians, lawyers, businessmen, and, after the Civil War, politicians . . . the conventions provide illuminating insight into the thinking of articulate blacks on the problems facing the race" such as slavery and the discrimination and "indignities" of the free colored folks (126).

20. To practice their traditional African ways would bring about cruel and unusual punishments, even death, considering that the African was, for the most part, under twenty-four hour surveillance in order to prevent insurrections. There is a debate amongst historians of slavery, who argue over the extent to which blacks within slavery had some form of autonomy. As can logically be deduced, the historians of the adaptive-vitality school (Blassingame, Gutman, Franklin, etc.) maintain that blacks were able to retain some of their African cultural heritage because they were to some extent autonomous. The historians of the pathological-pathogenic school (Elkins, Stampp, Genovese, etc.) argue to the contrary.

21. It should be noted that a debate lingers regarding the origins of African spirituality. Given that the Africans were prevented from establishing any institutions to reproduce their ethos in the colonies, I rather agree with E. Franklin Frazier's (1957) understanding:

> The most important institution which the Negro has built in the United States is the Negro church. Contrary to the claim of some students of the Negro that the Negro church was an African survival resurrected on American soil, the Negro church is a product of the American environment. The form of its organization and the character of its religious services were the result of the proselyting of Protestant missionaries, especially the Baptist and the Methodist missionaries. This does not mean that the Negro's peculiar experience in America did not contribute to the shaping of the institution. The influence of the Negro's experience in the building of his church is seen in the variations in the character of the Negro church, which reflect the extent of the Negro's education and isolation in American life and his economic and social status (87).

22. The character of the black family during slavery was so patterned after the institutional regulators of the American social structure that today there is talk of its disintegration resulting not from slavery, as E. Franklin Frazier (1939) proclaimed, but from the post-World War II public policies of welfare and job relocations out of urban, which has fostered female-headed households, teenage pregnancy, promiscuity, welfare dependency, out-of-wedlock births, etc. See William Julius Wilson's (1987) *The Truly Disadvantaged* and Herbert Gutman's (1976) *The Black Family in Slavery and Freedom*.

23. "As long as the slaves communed with whites [(and remained illiterate)], their religious instruction was circumscribed. The planters, in spite of their piety, insisted that their slaves not learn any of the potentially subversive tenets [(which whites themselves had used against their former masters, the English crown)] of Christianity (the brotherhood of all men, for instance)" (Blassingame, 1972: 61). Once the slaves learned these tenets, their quest for freedom became a fight for their "God" given rights.

24. See David R. Roediger's (1999) *The Wages of Whiteness: Race and the Making of the American Working Class*, as well as W.E.B. Du Bois's (1920) *Darkwater*, for an understanding of the impact race had in the construction of whiteness and its benefits.

25. Quoted in Hugh Tulloch, *The Debate on the American Civil War Era*, Manchester: Manchester University Press 1999, pp. 41.

26. This corroborates William Julius Wilson's (1978, 1987) thesis that race, as a determining factor for discrimination, is declining because the class factors of black existence are more relevant in discriminating against them than race, although, these class factors become conflated with the racial stereotypes, promiscuity, laziness, dependent, female-headed families, out-of-wedlock births, etc. which determined the black experience during slavery.

My point in evoking Wilson is to highlight two points in regard to this conflation: first, the fact that outside of the physical differences, only class distinction divides blacks from mainstream America (black and white middle-class groups). That is, once upper mobility is obtained, through education and professional occupations, there is no distinct black identity or consciousness. In fact, Wilson and others have pointed out that blacks, who become upwardly mobile through the attainment of higher education, assume acceptable mainstream behaviors. Which brings us to the second point, the response of Blacks to this conflation. Assimilated blacks, like Wilson, proffer public policy agendas for the "social isolation" of the black underclass which will foster mainstream values, job creations, and education over those welfare policies that exacerbate the culture of poverty, i.e. promiscuity, out-of-wedlock families, teenage pregnancy, dependency, female headed households, etc., which have developed as a result of attempting to exercise a reified consciousness focused on material accumulation in a material resource depleted environment, which again proves that black consciousness simply is the degree to which blacks attempt to exercise the reified consciousness of the American social structure, i.e., the Protestant Ethic, and its discursive praxis, the spirit of capitalism.

Chapter Three

On the Interpretation of Du Bois's Double Consciousness

William Edward Burghardt Du Bois (February 23, 1868–August 27, 1963) was born to Alfred Du Bois and Mary Silvina Burghardt Du Bois one year after the Fourteenth Amendment was ratified, and added to the US Constitution. After graduating from Fisk University (1888), Du Bois earned a bachelor's degree from Harvard, studied abroad in Berlin, and returned to Harvard where he became the first black American to earn a Ph.D. degree. He went on to teach at Wilberforce University in Ohio, the University of Pennsylvania, and Atlanta University where he established the department of sociology. The descendant of free people of color from the Caribbean and the North, Du Bois knew nothing of Africa or the South, until his Fisk years, and his encounters with discrimination and racism stems from the racial biases of his Protestant community toward the Scots-Irish, and his marginalization by a female schoolmate when he was in grade school.

Born and raised in the predominantly white Protestant community of Great Barrington, Massachusetts, Du Bois, was, as Cornel West (1996) points out,

> ... first and foremost a black New England Victorian seduced by the Enlightenment ethos and enchanted with the American Dream. His interpretation of the human condition—that is, in part, his idea of who he was and could be—was based on his experiences and, most importantly, on his understanding of those experiences through the medium of an Enlightenment worldview that promoted Victorian strategies in order to realize an American optimism. . . . Like many of the brilliant and ambitious young men of his time, he breathed the intoxicating fumes of "advanced" intellectual and political culture. . . . [This intellectual and political culture, however,] precluded his access to the distinctive black tragicomic sense and black encounter with the absurd. He certainly saw, analyzed, and empathized with black sadness, sorrow, and suffering. But he didn't feel it in his bones deeply enough, nor was he intellectually open enough to position

himself alongside the sorrowful, suffering, yet striving ordinary black folk. Instead, his own personal and intellectual distance lifted him above them even as he addressed their plight in his progressive writings. Du Bois was never alienated by black people—he lived in black communities where he received great respect and admiration. But there seemed to be something in him that alienated ordinary black people. In short, he was reluctant to learn fundamental lessons about life—and about himself—from them. Such lessons would have required that he—at least momentarily—believe that they were or might be as wise, insightful, and "advanced" as he; and this he could not do (58).

Du Bois could not see that "ordinary black people were or might be as wise, insightful, and advanced as he" precisely because he was an agent of the Protestant ethic and his times and therefore saw "ordinary black people," whose equality to whites he felt "lay in excellence in accomplishment" (Du Bois, 1968: 75), and their practical consciousness as a backward "other," held back not because of their racial difference, "innate love of harmony and beauty," but by "race prejudice." This "racial prejudice," unlike the majority of "ordinary black people," he was for the most part able to avoid growing up in the northern town of Great Barrington, Massachusetts where he was socialized. As Du Bois observes of his own upbringing,

> In general thought and conduct I became quite thoroughly New England. It was not good form in Great Barrington to express one's thoughts volubly, or to give way to excessive emotion. We were even sparing in our daily greetings. There was on the street only a curt "good morning" to those whom you knew well and no greetings at all from others. I am quite sure that in a less restrained and conventional atmosphere I should have easily learned to express my emotions with far greater and more unrestrained intensity; but as it was I had the social heritage not only of a New England clan but Dutch taciturnity. This was later reinforced and strengthened by inner withdrawals in the face of real and imagined discriminations. The result was that I was early thrown in upon myself. I found it difficult and even unnecessary to approach other people and by that same token my own inner life perhaps grew the richer; but the habit of repression often returned to plague me in after years, for so early a habit could not easily be unlearned. The Negroes in the South, when I came to know them, could never understand why I did not naturally greet everyone I passed on the street or slap my friends on the back (Du Bois, 1968: 93).

Thus, Du Bois, who experienced *little* race prejudice in his formative years (1868–1885) where he attended an all white Episcopalian church and school, like the rest of the black bourgeoisie during his lifetime, "the best of the house servants, [and] the educated free Negro from the North," who together numbered about 500, 000 "at the outbreak of the Civil War," became, and was, given his socialization, a bourgeois agent of the Protestant ethic whose understanding of the world and "others" was based on: "(1) monogamous nuclear family organization; (2) temperance and orderliness as behavioral principles, including thrift and internalization of disciplined work habits; (3) favorable disposition toward formal education and training in the ways of urban civilization; and (4) legitimation of class hierarchy within the racial community" (Reed, 1997: 28). Unlike many of his white and black Protestant bourgeois contemporaries, however, he does not view "the Negroes in the South," i.e., "ordinary black people," whom he saw as being distinct from his "New England and Dutch social heritage," in the structurally derogatory and antithetical Protestant terms (i.e., lazy, promiscuous, emotional, disorderly, etc.) of the larger white society; instead, "when he first came to know them," on a return trip from New Bedford, Massachusetts with his grandfather in 1883, Du Bois celebrates their distinctiveness, i.e., "otherness:"[1]

> ... I viewed with astonishment ten thousand Negroes of every hue and bearing, saw in open-mouthed astonishment the whole gorgeous gamut of the American Negro world; the swaggering men, the beautiful girls, the laughter and gaiety, the unhampered self-expression. I was astonished and inspired. I apparently noted nothing of poverty or degradation, but only extraordinary beauty of skin-color and utter equality of mien, with absence so far as I could see of even the shadow of the line of race (Du Bois, 1968: 99).

In songs and religious practices, Du Bois, when he attends Fisk for college in 1885, also becomes aware of that "unhampered self-expression" of blackness which made the Negro "community a world" distinct from his Puritan community:

> I heard the Negro folksong first in Great Barrington, sung by the Hampton Singers. But that was second-hand, sung by youth who never knew slavery. I now heard the Negro songs by those who made them and in the land of their American birth. It was in the village into which my country school district filtered of Saturdays and Sundays. The road wandered from our rambling log-house up the stony bed of a creek, past wheat and corn, until we could hear dimly across the fields a rhythmic cadence of song—soft, thrilling, powerful, that swelled and died sorrowfully in our ears. I had never seen a Southern Negro revival. To be sure, we in Berkshire were not perhaps as stiff and formal as they in Suffolk, of olden time; yet we were very quiet and subdued, and I know not what would have happened those clear Sabbath mornings had someone punctuated the sermon with a scream, or interrupted the long prayer with a loud Amen!
> And so most striking to me, as I approached the village and the little plain church perched aloft, was the air of intense excitement that possessed that mass of black folk. A sort of suppressed terror hung in the air and seemed to seize them—a pythian madness, a demoniac possession, that lent terrible reality to song and word. The black and massive form of the preacher swayed and quivered as

the words crowded to his lips and flew at us in singular eloquence. The people moaned and fluttered, and then the gaunt-cheeked brown woman beside me suddenly leaped straight into the air and shrieked like a lost soul, while round about came wail and groan and outcry, and a scene of human passion such as I had never conceived before (Du Bois, 1968: 120).

Thus, at Fisk, Du Bois, through their emotionalism, spiritualism, and music, encounters "a" black, folk, underclass, world, which differed from his middle class upbringing, and embraces it,

I have called my community a world, and so its isolation made it. There was among us but a half-awakened common consciousness, sprung from common joy and grief, at burial, birth or wedding; from a common hardship in poverty, poor land and low wages; and, above all, from the sight of the Veil that hung between us and Opportunity (Du Bois, 1968:120).

"The Fisk years" (1885–1888), as Julius Lester (1971) suggests, "were the beginning. He came there an American looking for blackness; he left, having become aware of that blackness" (12):

I forgot, or did not thoroughly realize, the curious irony by which I was not looked upon as a real citizen of my birth-town, with a future and a career, and instead was being sent to a far land among strangers who were regarded as (and in truth were) "mine own people" (Du Bois, 2003 [1920]: 42).

So I came to a region where the world was split into white and black halves, and where the darker half was held back by race prejudice and legal bonds, as well as by deep ignorance and dire poverty. But facing this was not a lost group, but at Fisk a microcosm of a world and a civilisation in potentiality. Into this world I leapt with enthusiasm. A new loyalty and allegiance replaced my Americanism: hence-forward I was a Negro (Du Bois, 1986 [1968]: 108).

The net result of the Fisk interlude was to broaden the scope of my program of life, not essentially to change it; to center it in a group of educated Negroes, who from their knowledge and experience would lead the mass. I never for a moment dreamed that such leadership could ever be for the sake of the educated group itself, but always for the mass. Nor did I pause to enquire in just what ways and with what technique we would work—first, broad, exhaustive knowledge of the world; all other wisdom, all method and application would be added unto us. In essence I combined a social program for a depressed group with the natural demand of youth for "Light, more light" (Du Bois, 1986 [1968]: 123).

Clearly, in his early thoughts and actions, Du Bois (as these quotes demonstrate) is aware of an overt difference between his upbringing, demeanor, and overall outlook on life, which he deems Americanism, and "the unhampered self-expression" of a group of strangers in the South who were regarded as his own people. Why and how, then, is "double consciousness" in *The Souls of Black Folk* (1903) the sign of the racial and national distinctiveness of black culture and character, biculturalism, characterized by Du Bois's Americanism and this "unhampered self-expression," i.e., "emotionalism" and "spiritual and musical ideals"? Why is the "unhampered self-expression" of black folk not merely the dissolution and reformulation of Du Bois's Americanism, among a segregated and "isolated" minority (i.e., "depressed group"), hampered by the material conditions (i.e., "hardship in poverty," "poor land and low wages," "race prejudice and legal bonds," and "ignorance and dire poverty"), "barbarism," and relational logic of the South or that same Americanism?

The answer to these two questions is simple. Du Bois, the father of pan-African bourgeois nationalism led by the "Talented Tenth" of the race, by the time he publishes *The Souls of Black Folk* (1903), which is a collection of fourteen essays previously published during the early years of his life, has both a racial deterministic and sociocultural view of race mediated by the late nineteenth and early twentieth century concept of nation, which turned the "spiritual idealism and musical style" of the isolated black, underclass, community into their African "innate love of harmony and beauty" which relationally made them racially and nationally distinct from their white counterparts:

> But while race differences have followed mainly physical race lines, yet no mere physical distinctions would really define or explain the deeper differences, the cohesiveness, and continuity of these groups. The deeper differences are spiritual, psychical, differences—undoubtedly based on the physical, but infinitely transcending them. The forces that bind together the Teuton nations are, then, first, their race identity and common blood; secondly, and more important, a common history, common laws and religion, similar habits of thought and a conscious striving together for certain ideals of life. The whole process which has brought about these race differentiations has been a growth, and the great characteristic of this growth has been the differentiation of spiritual and mental differences between great races of mankind and the integration of physical differences. . . . Here, it seems to me, is the reading of the riddle that puzzles so many of us. We are Americans, not only by birth and by citizenship, but by our political ideals, our language, our religion. Farther than that our Americanism does not go. At that point we are Negroes, members of a vast historic race that from the very dawn of creation has slept, but half awakens in the dark forests of its African fatherland. We are the first fruits of this new nation, the harbinger of that black tomorrow which is yet destined to soften the whiteness of the Teutonic today. We are that people whose subtle sense of song has given America its only American music, its only American fairy tales, its only touch of pathos and humor amid its money-getting plutocracy. As such, it is our duty to conserve

our physical powers, our intellectual endowments, our spiritual ideals; as a race we must strive by race organization, by race solidarity, by race unity to the realization of that broader humanity which freely recognizes differences in men, but sternly deprecates inequality in their opportunities of development (Du Bois, 1971 [1897]: 179–183).

This 1897 passage, published the same year as "Of Our Spiritual Strivings" where Du Bois first conceptualized the double consciousness construct, highlights Du Bois's nineteenth-century racial understanding of consciousness formation as mediated by the concepts of race and nation, which he would apply to his understanding of who he was and who the rest of black America was. Du Bois, as his autobiographies read, was completely embroiled in the "white Americanism" of Great Barrington, albeit racially distinct because of his physical difference, "black blood," until he goes to Fisk where he encounters the "spiritual" and "psychical" strivings of his "undoubtedly" physical difference—"Then of course, when I went South to Fisk, I became a member of a closed racial group with rites and loyalties, with a history and a corporate future, with an art and philosophy." Building on late nineteenth and early twentieth century notions of racialism and nationalism, which focused on drawing boundaries between nation-states and racial bodies that marked national "insiders" and "outsiders," Du Bois utilized the idea of race as a substance both biological and spiritual (the "souls" of black folk) to inscribe black folk in a temporal community, black nation, defined by its "doubleness," American and Negro. The former characterized by its civilization and "enlightenment" ethos, the latter by its emotionalism and spiritualism. In other words, whites, the Teuton nation, were characterized by their rationality and temperance, and blacks, southern blacks, were characterized by their emotionalism, spiritualism, and musical style.

Alienated from both groups—the larger society because of his "black blood," and black America because his education and "social heritage" detached him from their "unfortunate" experiences—however, Du Bois ambivalently sought refuge in uplifting the latter (to his status position) in order to voice what he saw, through the prism of race and nation, as their distinct (racial and national) voice or soul, i.e., religiosity and music (stemming from Africa), without bleaching it "in a flood of white Americanism," i.e., his Enlightenment (status) ethos:

> Here, then, is the dilemma, and it is a puzzling one, I admit. No Negro who has given earnest thought to the situation of his people in America has failed, at some time in life, to find himself at these crossroads; has failed to ask himself at some time, "What, after all, am I? Am I an American or am I a Negro? Can I be both? Or is it my duty to cease to be a Negro as soon as possible and be

an American? If I strive as a Negro, am I not perpetuating the very cleft that threatens and separates black and white America? Is not my only possible practical aim the subduction of all that is Negro in me to the American? Does my black blood place upon me any more obligation to assert my nationality than German, or Irish or Italian blood would?" . . . [I]t is our duty to conserve our physical powers, our intellectual endowments, our spiritual ideals; as a race we must strive by race organization, by race solidarity, by race unity to the realization of that broader humanity which freely recognizes differences in men, but sternly deprecates inequality in their opportunities of development (Du Bois, 1971 [1897]: 182–183).

Clearly, the late nineteenth and early twentieth century "discourse of blood, skin colour and cross-breeding" (Balibar, 1991: 207) concealed Du Bois's ambivalence, and shaped his understanding of his "black identity" as a double consciousness, a bicultural form of being-in-the-world that distinguished and alienated him from *both* black and white America:

After the Egyptian and Indian, the Greek and Roman, the Teuton and Mongolian, the Negro is a sort of seventh son, born with a veil, and gifted with second-sight in this American world, —a world which yields him no true self-consciousness, but only lets him see himself through the revelation of the other world. It is a peculiar sensation, this double-consciousness, this sense of always looking at one's self through the eyes of others, of measuring one's soul by the tape of a world that looks on in amused contempt and pity. One ever feels his twoness, —an American, a Negro; two souls, two thoughts, two unreconciled strivings; two warring ideals in one dark body, whose dogged strength alone keeps it from being torn asunder.

The history of the American Negro is the history of this strife, —this longing to attain self conscious manhood, to merge his double self into a better and truer self. In this merging he wishes neither of the older selves to be lost. He would not Africanize America, for America has too much to teach the world and Africa. He would not bleach his Negro soul in a flood of white Americanism, for he knows that Negro blood has a message for the world. He simply wishes to make it possible for a man to be both a Negro and an American, without being cursed and spit upon by his fellows, without having the doors of Opportunity closed roughly in his face (Du Bois, 1995 [1903]: 43–47).

As is clearly outlined from this often-quoted conception of "double consciousness" in *The Souls of Black Folk*, Du Bois's take is not that the black American is only an American (upper middle class sensibility) hampered by the poverty and racial prejudice of the South or the "other world," as I am suggesting and to which Du Bois admittedly alludes to in his later (1968) autobiographical writings; on the contrary, in *The Souls of Black Folk* he is suggesting that the Black American's consciousness is divided between two distinct epistemologies and ontologies—"two souls, two thoughts"—one African (Negro), with its own "innate messages" stemming from his "Negro blood," and the other white (American).

If Du Bois by the time he penned *The Souls of Black Folk* has fully transcended the racial and national ideology of the late nineteenth and early twentieth century, to offer a sociohistorical understanding of black consciousness, what is the role of this talk about 'blood' and 'Teuton' nation? This question is a moot point. For the problem for Du Bois in the above-mentioned passages is not the concept of blood and nation as the basis for the constitution of black consciousness, which he clearly accepts. The problem for Du Bois is the "peculiar sensation;" that the "African World" is structurally revealed to the African "through the revelation of the other world," which "looks on in amused contempt and pity" and prevents the "Negro" from reconciling their "twoness," given the juxtaposition of the two "physical" worlds in diametrical opposition to one another (White is civilized, Black is barbaric, etc.).

It is this ambivalent estrangement or strife, the desire "to attain self conscious manhood" and reject the contempt to which they are subject, produced by the society's structural ("class racism") differentiation, which Du Bois subscribes to, that Du Bois captures with his racialized and nationalized double consciousness construct. The construct, as such, does not, however, without relying on their "innate love of harmony and beauty," articulate the sociohistorical nature of all black practical consciousness or identity. It instead highlights the liberal bourgeois (ideological class) basis of the construct as supplemented by race: the desire of the liberal black Protestant heterosexual bourgeois male to seek equality of opportunity, distribution, and recognition in the American capitalist social milieu amidst their contempt for that milieu because they are "cursed and spitted" upon and prevented from achieving that equality or integration justified through the prism of the same ideology they subscribe to and desperately seek to reproduce. It is this purposive-rationale Du Bois captures with his construct against the conservative bourgeois economism of Booker T. Washington, who sought economic gain for the black masses in a separate and racial position of their own, and the black nationalism of Marcus Garvey.

In order to capture this ambivalent estrangement, which conceals the ideological interest (desire to obtain equality of distribution and recognition) of the liberal black Protestant bourgeois male, who have come to be the bearers of ideological domination in "black America," it is necessary to apply my structural understanding of the constitution of the American body polity to the constitution of Du Bois's own liberal bourgeois Protestant consciousness and understanding of consciousness formation in order to deconstruct his "doubleness" ideology.

Whereas I am suggesting that historically "the revelation of this world," the American (upper-middle class and racist) social structure, forced African consciousness to assume the agential moments of the American world's practical consciousness, for the Du Bois of the *Souls*, which views the constitution of consciousness through both physical and cultural processes as mediated by the bourgeois ideology of nationalism, this "revelation" does not efface the "doubleness" (African and American) of the "souls" or consciousness of black folks; but makes it difficult for them to reconcile the "two thoughts" in order for them to be in the American social world. That is, for the Du Bois of *The Souls*, the differentiated and divergent social behaviors of the Negro from white America are part of his "innate sense of blackness," or "Negro blood," and the aim of the Negro is "to merge his double self into a better and truer self. In this merging he wishes neither of the older selves to be lost. He would not Africanize America, for America has too much to teach the world and Africa. He would not bleach his Negro soul in a flood of white Americanism, for he knows that Negro blood has a message for the world. He simply wishes to make it possible for a man to be both a Negro and an American, without being cursed and spit upon by his fellows, without having the doors of opportunity closed roughly in his face."

This is Du Boisian double consciousness as a reference to black American biculturalism as we have come to understand it in the social sciences. It is my position, however, that the construct does not adequately capture the sociohistorical nature of black American consciousness; rather it captures and speaks to Du Bois's ambivalence towards the American nation-state and his purposive-rationale, to recursively organize and reproduce the Protestant ethic of the society in order to obtain equality of opportunity, distribution, and recognition for all black folks amidst racial and class discrimination produced by the logic of the very consciousness he seeks to recursively organize and reproduce for blacks. Within the language of nineteenth-century racial ideology Du Bois's ambivalence in the Souls comes off as an argument for black American biculturalism. However, deconstructed from its racial and national ideology, the construct is not really a reference to biculturalism; it instead highlights the aforementioned ambivalence. Let me elaborate. From my understanding of the constitution of black consciousness through disavowal, or the relational logic of my structuralism, the former slaves, as interpellated "other" agents of the social structure, at the moment of antagonism in the American world's "ideological apparatuses," construct and constructed their consciousness, like their white counterparts, by warring against the ideals and practices associated with the "other" for the "pure" practical consciousness of authority, not because, as Du Bois points out, they were trying to reconcile these two racial and national "souls" into one distinct consciousness, but in order to be in the socially constructed American capitalist racial world and reject the contempt to which they are subject. In Du Boisian terms, "He simply wishes to make it possible for a man to be both a Negro and an American, without being cursed and spit upon by his fellows, without having the doors of opportunity closed roughly in his face." That is, the majority of the slaves attempted to live up to what master signifies as proper human conduct against the un-human-like qualities that is or was master's representation of the former slave as an "other."

This does not mean that the consciousness of the slave, as an African, was or is obliterated, or for that matter is a pathological reaction to whites, as a result of the slavery process (Myrdal, 1944; Liebow, 1967; Berger, 1967), only that the master, through the production and reproduction of the representation of Africanness in and through their ideological apparatuses, used the African's very own initial practical consciousness against them to legitimate the relationship that delimits their "pure" non-African social structure and material practice.

In other words, the African survivals—in courtship practices, dance, familial roles, folktales, language, music, names, proverbs, and religious beliefs and practice (Herskovits, 1941; Karenga, 1993; Holloway, 1990)—initially practiced by the Africans were mirrored back to them as negative ways of Being (ungodly, licentious, emotional, irrational, uncivilized, etc.), which in relation to that of white Americanism (godly, pious, obedient, pure, civilized, rational, diligent, etc.) were un-human-like, and which laws of the American capitalist "ideological mechanical solidarity" prohibited them from practicing.

Du Bois's argument in *The Souls*, by relying on the reference to "Negro blood" as mediated by the concept of nation, is that this relationship gives the "Negroes" an invariant "twoness" for understanding reality: the practical consciousness they begin and began with (in his view their "innate" African spirituality, and "love of harmony and beauty"), as it is or was mirrored back to them from the master, and the "pure" practical consciousness of the master. Thus the "twoness" Du Bois alludes to, in this understanding, is between two opposing ontologies, African and white American, grounded in both cultural processes and physical differences, which when synthesized yields not only a new ontology, but also a new epistemological mode of knowing and constructing reality.

My structural reading diametrically opposes this racialized "double" episteme take of Du Bois and many of his later liberal nationalist or culturalist followers (Gilroy, 1993; West, 1993; Allen, 2001) who want to hold on to his concept to explain black identity as somehow distinct from that of the American one because of their "improvisational communalism," "musical and spiritual ideals," or "excitement and emotionalism" as seen by conservatives (Sowell, 1975, 1981; Murray, 1984); instead, the validity of Du Bois's construct lies in the fact that it highlights the "class racism" of the black identity that for so long served as the bearers of ideological domination for the "race."

My view is that black consciousness is not singular and homogenized defined by its dualism; instead within the American Protestant liberal bourgeois male social structure it (black American consciousness) became multiple and diverse, differentially related to and dominated by those blacks (upper and middle class blacks) who have internalized the protestant ethic of the American capitalist world as their practical consciousness against all other adaptive responses (i.e., black communism, tribalism, homosexuality, feminism, etc.), which they assessed in terms of the "racial class" basis of the society. It is in reference to their (liberal black bourgeoisie or middle class) being-in-the-world that Du Bois's double consciousness has its validity.

To understand this position better, let us look at it from my structural perspective by applying my theoretical understanding of consciousness formation to the development of Du Bois's own consciousness, and extrapolating his experiences as the historical norm for a particular group of black folks, i.e., the liberal black Protestant heterosexual male bourgeoisie, who, like Du Bois, internalized the middle class/racial protestant ideology of the American social structure.

Again my understanding of consciousness formation revealed in the previous chapter posits that it is the legal regulations of a society, its "lexicons and representations of signification," its rules of conduct that are sanctioned (as outlined by the power elites) which represents the objective conditions (social structure) of society that structures social relations and constitutes the "ideological" materials by which consciousness is recursively organized and reproduced in material practice as "practical-consciousness."

The general understanding is that individual actors (irreducibly situated subjects) are relationally socialized within society—its semiotic field or predefined and predetermined lexicons and representations of signification, i.e., the field of socialization "and its investment in reproducing and naturalising the structures of power" (Slemon, 1995:47). This socialization takes place through "ideological apparatuses," which in American society represent an ideological flanking for the protestant ethic and the spirit of capitalism, controlled by socialized institutional regulators. The relation between the two runs this way: societal power operates through a complex relationship between ideological apparatuses (i.e., the law, education, rituals, family etc.) and institutional regulators who appropriate and manufacture lexicons and representations of signification of individuals in order to consolidate and legitimate society as a natural "order" and to reproduce individuals as deployable units of that order.

This does not mean that the individuals in the social order are determined by the ideology of those in power positions in society; on the contrary, what is implied is that social actors construct their identities and practical consciousnesses in relation to the representations of those in power positions. They can choose to do what ever they want to do or be, but this is always at the expense of, and to, their ontological security.

Understanding the development of Du Bois's consciousness within the framework of this theoretical model, Du Bois, as an irreducibly situated subject, is an interpellated subject, a constituting unit of the American Protestant "class racial" social structure. Du Bois is socialized through ideological apparatuses, i.e., an Episcopalian family, the Episcopalian church of his youth, at Fisk, Harvard, Berlin, etc., in the society's (reified consciousness) semiotic field established by institutional regulators who, on the one hand, subscribe to an Enlightenment ethos, "enframed" by the purposive-rationality of the Protestant ethic, as mediated by the concept of nation for themselves (insiders); and, on the other hand, structurally prescribe ("other outsiders")an unchanging subhuman condition for Du Bois and people who look like him given their skin color and alleged inferior intellect, justified through that same "racial class" ideological ethos, i.e., whites are rational, civilized, etc., and blacks are sophomoric, emotional, barbarous, etc.

Du Bois's eccentricity as a structurally differentiated, discriminated against black "other outsider" "is his driving ambition to excel intellectually and psychologically to become 'a fellow of Harvard'" (Bell, 1996: 98), and recursively reproduce the "pure" agential moments of his society in spite of the ideas and practices (i.e., segregation, prejudice, etc.) stemming from Harvard and the American world around him, which suggest he cannot on account of his "physical" racial inferiority:

> At Fisk, the problem of race was faced openly and essential racial equality asserted and natural inferiority strenuously denied. In some cases the teachers expressed this theory; in most cases the student opinion naturally forced it. At Harvard, on the other hand, I began to face scientific race dogma: first of all, evolution and the "Survival of the Fittest." It was continually stressed in the community and in classes that there was a vast difference in the development of the whites and the "lower" races; that this could be seen in the physical development of the Negro. . . .
>
> I do not know how I came first to form my theories of race. The process was probably largely unconscious. The differences of personal appearance between me and my fellows, I must have been conscious of when quite young. Whatever distinctions came because of that did not irritate me; they rather exalted me because, on the whole, while I was still a youth, they gave me exceptional position and a chance to excel rather than handicapping me.

Then of course, when I went South to Fisk, I became a member of a closed racial group with rites and loyalties, with a history and a corporate future, with an art and philosophy. I received these eagerly and expanded them so that when I came to Harvard the theory of race separation was quite in my blood. I did not seek contact with my white fellow students. On the whole I rather avoided them. I took it for granted that we were training ourselves for different careers in worlds largely different. There was not the slightest idea of the permanent subordination and inequality of my world. Nor again was there any idea of racial amalgamation. I resented the assumption that we desired it (Du Bois, 1984 [1940]: 97–101).

In this framework, accordingly, Du Bois is an interpellated discriminated against minority, a member of a structurally differentiated "class-in-itself," blacks, within the American ideological mechanical solidarity, who is attempting to be a "coworker in the kingdom of culture" as defined by the institutional regulators, rich, white, protestant men, of his society. He is prevented from doing so, becoming an institutional regulator in the larger American society, because of race and class prejudice (i.e., structural differentiation), which indexed him with all blacks, the majority of whom, according to Du Bois, were lowly and backward because they were handicapped by race prejudice, ignorance, and dire poverty.

Alienated from both groups, whites because he is black and the majority of blacks because he lacks their emotionalism, improvisation, and musical styles, Du Bois seeks, "through the leadership of men like myself" (i.e., his pan-African bourgeois nationalist "Talented Tenth"), to define and apply his own cultural background (New England Way) to his segregated "poor" race or nation in America who do not have a double consciousness, but are characterized, according to Du Bois, by their "Africanism," i.e., emotionalism and spiritualism:

> For this group [(the Negroes or blacks)] I built my plan of study and accomplishment. Through the leadership of men like myself and my fellows, we were going to have these enslaved Israelites out of the still enduring bondage in short order. It was a battle which might conceivably call for force, but I could think of it mainly as a battle of wits; of knowledge and deed, which by sheer reason and desert, must eventually overwhelm the forces of hate, ignorance and reaction (Du Bois, 1968: 112–113).

Thus, the early Du Bois, consciously and unconsciously, accepts the structurally differentiated racial and class understandings of the social structure, and recursively reproduces its "pure" ethics in his praxis through the prisms of his liberal bourgeois black national Protestantism. That is, Du Bois wants to be a fellow at Harvard in order to acquire (through solipsistic hard work) the knowledge, class and status position, which will allow him to be a "coworker in the kingdom of culture" through his deeds based on that knowledge. However, Du Bois is (as a discriminated against minority) also ambivalent about Harvard and the American cultural world because of their racial ideas, which keep the majority of his "group" unequal to whites and enslaved as a structurally differentiated "class-in-itself" known as blacks, who have a distinct consciousness because of their emotionalism and spiritualism stemming from their "black blood." At the moment of antagonism, as an "other," within the American "other world," which is paradoxically also his world, Du Bois shuns it to build a plan of study and accomplishment (pan-African bourgeois nationalism as led by their "Talented Tenth") for "the Negroes," who lack his "otherworldly" class training acquired from Harvard and growing up in Great Barrington.

It is this ambivalence, the desire to "excel" and reject the contempt to which he is subject, Du Bois, using late nineteenth and early twentieth century racial science and ideology, captures with the notion of biculturalism or double consciousness. This reference is merely perspectival and ideological, concealing Du Bois's racial class interest amidst the discriminatory affects of American society: to define and prove black self-worth along the purposive-rationale of obtaining equality of opportunity and recognition in the larger American society. In other words, Du Bois's ambivalence does not bless him with two distinct epistemologies or ontologies, as his double consciousness construct by relying on the racial and national ideology of the late nineteenth and early twentieth century reads.

There are no African structural institutions (Fisk, during Du Bois's stance, was dominated by white teachers—with the exception of one black, William Morris—"from New England or from the New Englandized Middle West")[2] from which Du Bois would have interpretively developed an African ethos. His only understanding of African is revealed to him through the discriminatory identifications of institutional regulators of the "other world" (his world), at Harvard, and the fully visible agential moments of those, i.e., the poor blacks at Fisk, who recursively appear to reproduce the discriminatory identity (i.e., their "emotionalism" and "innate love of harmony and beauty") that delimited the white world his teachers at Fisk were teaching or applying to the Negroes in the South.

Instead, the ambivalence places Du Bois in a "liminal space" wherein alternative meanings and practices from that of his society may arise, given that the ideals of power are revealed to be something that they are not, socially constructed as opposed to natural. In the case of Du Bois, however, the ambivalence produced homogenization or the drive for equality of opportunity, distribution, and recognition, i.e., "to attain self-conscious manhood . . .

without being cursed and spit upon by his fellows, without having the doors of Opportunity closed roughly in his face."

In Bhabhaian terms, in other words, the assumption of the "pure" ideals of authority, "class racism," which Du Bois recursively organizes and reproduces as liberal pan-African bourgeois nationalism led by the Talented Tenth of the race constructing a plan of study for blacks "to attain self conscious manhood," i.e., equality of distribution and recognition, along the lines of: "(1) monogamous nuclear family organization; (2) temperance and orderliness as behavioral principles, including thrift and internalization of disciplined work habits; (3) favorable disposition toward formal education and training in the ways of urban civilization; and (4) legitimation of class hierarchy within the racial community" (Reed, 1997: 28). Thus Du Bois does not really seek to define black consciousness, but within this perspectival and ideological foundation or purposive-rationale he seeks to institutionalize blacks in the American social formation.

In sum, the institutional regulators (rich, white, Protestant men) of Dr. Du Bois's era subscribe to the ethos of equality among men, exercising their God given inalienable rights to pursue freely economic gain for its own sake in a particular "calling." They maintain and recursively organize these ideas aided by racial slavery and Jim Crow segregation, justifying them by pointing to the inferiority and inhumanity of the non-white Africans, who possess an "identity-in-differential" to the civilized whites because of their emotionalism and innate sense of blackness. These ideas and practices are taught in the home, are codified in the laws, and are subsequently justified by scientific dogma and evidence (Social Darwinism), which is published and taught in schools or the ideological apparatuses of the society.

Dr. Du Bois is not exempt from these ideas given his Protestant New England Victorian upbringing and Harvard education, which made him a typical son of the Enlightenment (Black Anglo Saxon Protestant) like his white counterparts, "who viewed society [(and the world at-large)] largely through the prism of [(Protestant)] ethics and spirituality" (Marable, 1986: 51). What differentiates Du Bois from his white counterparts, however, is his black skin, which did not prevent him from becoming an institutional regulator, i.e., he was an Atlanta University professor and longtime editor of the NAACP's *Crisis*, but (from the position of the white power elites) this indexed him with all blacks as a subordinate racial class-in-itself.

It should be mentioned, that Du Bois as a structurally differentiated discriminated against "other," does not, given his phenomenological meditation, initially come up with a different "form of orientation in the world"; again, he is an "other" because of race and class prejudice or structural differentiation, which prevents him from living as an institutional regulator within the larger society. Du Bois, in practically every respect, subscribes to the understanding of the "other world," but wants their substantive values—"for the words I longed for, and all their dazzling opportunities, were theirs, not mine. But they should not keep these prizes, I said; some, all, I would wrest from them"—for his kind, i.e., black folk, who were poor not because of the "innateness" of the negative stereotypes revealed by the "other world," which for Du Bois they (not him) clearly demonstrated, but because they were unfortunate, which Du Bois, as an agent of the Protestant ethic believed, "could easily be mended by thrift and sacrifice," "knowledge," and "accomplishment."

This is the estrangement, outside of the racial and national ideology of the 19th century, explicitly embedded in the construct, that gives rise to Dr. Du Bois's (as a paragon for his class, i.e., the black bourgeoisie) "double consciousness" construct, and makes it distinct, for example, from the Marxist scholar Antonio Gramsci's "two theoretical consciousnesses." Du Bois's ideology and experience is rooted in the structure of meaning and reference that is the semiotic field of his society. That is, Du Bois's initial agency, and hence his ambivalence, results from structural contradictions. Du Bois's subjective position is a result of the power and resistance of one hegemonic historical bloc, which he initially opposes "by convicting it [(the ideals of upper-middle class Americanism) of nonidentity with itself" (Adorno, 1973 [1966]: 147), not by positing a differing ontology or epistemology.

Gramsci's "two theoretical consciousnesses," on the contrary, imply that the social actor is divided between two hegemonic articulatory principles, one practical and the other ideal with its own articulatory principles. Du Bois's ideals and practices, which stem from the articulatory principles of one historical bloc, are one and the same, which, under the purview of late nineteenth and early twentieth century social thought that prevented racial integration, became for Du Bois liberal pan-African bourgeois nationalism as led by the "Talented Tenth" of the black race seeking equality of opportunity, distribution, and recognition for black folk in order to reject the contempt to which they were subject.

Du Bois is not seeking to institute into the American social world an alternative consciousness, or non-identity that opposes his American bourgeois liberal Protestantism. Instead, Du Bois responds to the paradox of being ideologically a bourgeois middle class American (although he understood most of the ideas to be universal), with no other ideals/practices to exercise in the world, and yet his existence is negated by the rationale of this same ideology by convicting the American social structure of nonidentity with itself. (As Du Bois tells us, "I was blithely European and imperialist in outlook; democratic as democracy was conceived in America" (Du Bois, 1984 [1968]: 32). Du Bois chose to address the institutional regulators of the American mechanical solidarity, given their negative representation of him and people who looked like him, because they subordinated "the will and well being of blacks individually and collectively to those of the dominant group" (Bell, 1996: 92). He wanted democracy and economic gain for his people.[3] His aim was, since "there is substantial agreement in laws, language and religion . . . there is a satisfactory adjustment of economic life . . ." (Du Bois, 1971 [1897]: 182), for the men of the two races to strive together for their "race ideals" rather "than in isolation," which the racist signifiers of the society attempted to prevent for the majority of blacks, who remained a class-in-itself, not because they had an identity-in-differential to that of whites, but due to structural differentiation, i.e., Jim Crow laws and worldwide racial prejudice backed by "scientific evidence":

> The absolute equality of races—physical, political and social—is the founding stone of world peace and human advancement. No one denies great differences of gift, capacity and attainment among individuals of all races, but the voice of science, religion and practical politics is one in denying the God-appointed existence of super-races, or of races naturally and inevitably and eternally inferior.
>
> That in the vast range of time, one group should in its industrial technique, or social organization, or spiritual vision, lag a few hundred years behind another, or forge fitfully ahead, or come to differ decidedly in thought, deed and ideal, is proof of the essential richness and variety of human nature, rather than proof of the co-existence of demi-gods and apes in human form. The doctrine of racial equality does not interfere with individual liberty, rather, it fulfils it. And of all the various criteria by which masses of men have in the past been prejudged and classified, that of the color of the skin and texture of the hair, is surely the most adventitious and idiotic (Du Bois, 1997 [1921]: 41).

Du Bois, as this passage highlights, wants the "ideological universals," i.e., sovereignty, equality, justice, the democratic and economic ideals etc., of his society for his race, which he sees (as "lowly," "backward," "ignorant and poor," etc., not because of their innate characteristics but as a result of social discrimination) through the light of his recursively organized and reproduced protestant bourgeois liberal ideology. He wants equality of opportunity, recognition and distribution for his race, "the backward and suppressed groups of mankind," which will be achieved, once discrimination is abandoned, through self-control, self knowledge, intelligence, and the help of their intelligentsia:

> It is the duty of the world to assist in every way the advance of the backward and suppressed groups of mankind. The rise of all men is a menace to no one and is the highest human ideal; it is not an altruistic benevolence, but the one road to world salvation.

> For the purpose of raising such peoples to intelligence, self-knowledge and self-control, their intelligentsia of right ought to be recognized as the natural leaders of their groups.
>
> The insidious and dishonorable propaganda, which, for selfish ends, so distorts and denies facts as to represent the advancement and development of certain races of men as impossible and undesirable, should be met with widespread dissemination of the truth. The experiment of making the Negro slave a free citizen in the United States is not a failure; the attempts at autonomous government in Haiti and Liberia are not proofs of the impossibility of self-government among black men; the experience of Spanish America does not prove that mulatto democracy will not eventually succeed there; the aspirations of Egypt and India are not successfully to be met by sneers at the capacity of darker races.
>
> We who resent the attempt to treat civilized men as uncivilized, and who bring in our hearts grievance upon grievance against those who lynch the untried, disfranchise the intelligent, deny self-government to educated men, and insult the helpless, we complain; but not simply or primarily for ourselves—more especially for the millions of our fellows, blood of our blood, and flesh of our flesh, who have not even what we have—the power to complain against monstrous wrong, the power to see and to know the source of our oppression (Du Bois, 1997 [1921]: 41–42).

The "double consciousness," then, deconstructed from its racial ideology as mediated by the concept of nation is not the sign of the distinctiveness of "Negro" culture and character; rather it is the ambivalence Du Bois (whose life represents a paragon of black bourgeois life) feels being ideologically American (upper middle class) yet being denied the fruits of this ideal in material practice because of the lowly representation of his "racial class" status, which he must war against to prove his humanity by recursively organizing and reproducing the structural "pure" terms of authority. In short, the construct is the embodiment of Du Bois's "class racism" as a black Protestant liberal nationalist, Du Bois desires for his race and nation the bourgeois ideals of the "spirit of capitalism" in order to reject the contempt to which blacks as second class citizens are subject. He advocates, in the face of racial discrimination, for the "educated" elites ("The Talented Tenth") of the black nation ("pan-Africanism) throughout the world to establish "Negro" institutions "for the purpose of raising such peoples to intelligence, self-knowledge and self-control." Du Bois makes this ambivalence clear when he writes at the tender age of ninety: "that dichotomy which all my life has characterized my thought: how far can love for my oppressed race accord with love for the oppressing country? And when these loyalties diverge, where shall my soul find refuge" (Du Bois, 1986[1968]: 169).

Consequently, it was the despair of being in this unremitting "ambivalent space"—"[t]he colored people of America are coming to face the fact quite calmly that most white Americans do not like them, and are planning neither for their survival, nor for their definite future if it involves free, self assertive modern manhood" (Du Bois, 1971 [1935]: 401)—, and Du Bois's continual "phenomenological meditation" on his social situation that leads him, in his controversial article "A Negro Nation Within the Nation" published in June 1935, to reject the sedimented and codified structures of signification of his American world, for another form of orientation in the world, i.e., black communism led by its "Talented tenth," which in the order of early twentieth-century anti-communist social life made him an "other" again.[4] The rest of black America, Du Bois, in his last autobiography, written in exile in Ghana, argues, have chosen to "follow [(as agents of the Protestant ethic, and its practice the spirit of capitalism)] in the footsteps of western acquisitive society, with its exploitation of labor, its monopoly of land and resources, and with private profit for the smart and unscrupulous in a world of poverty, disease, and ignorance, as the natural end of human culture." This predatory and soul-less end he argued, the black people of the world, as a collective led by "the advanced [(i.e., predestined)] guard of Negro people" (i.e., black people in America), should have avoided:

> Refuse to be cajoled or to change your way of life so as to make a few of your fellows rich at the expense of a mass of workers growing poor and sick, and remaining without schools so that a few black men can have automobiles.
> Africa here is a real danger which you must avoid or return to the slavery from which you are emerging.[5]

Barack Obama, contemporarily, like most blacks of the society, have not heeded this warning of Du Bois, to become a radical communist fighting against a liberal bourgeois Protestantism that fosters global class inequality and misery for the majority of people of color around the world; instead, Obama, in adopting the liberal bourgeois Protestantism ideology of the American polity has reintroduced the same ambivalent struggles Du Bois faced early on in his life, i.e., the struggle for equality of opportunity and recognition, by exercising the discursive practice of the society, amidst the discriminatory affects stemming from the ideals of the society, which has the majority of people of color exploited and oppressed. Whereas, Du Bois's struggle takes place in which racial worldviews and categories dominated the society, Obama's struggle takes place within an American liberal bourgeois Protestant new world order within which race is significantly declining as a threat to the life chances of blacks. In fact, the contrary is the case, the commodification of race and racial worldviews in the contemporary post-industrial American liberal bourgeois Protestant body-polity has become a significant factor in determining the life chances of blacks as they must attempt to adopt the social structural roles, athletes, entertainers, etc., assigned for blacks in the society, as a sign of their predestination, while avoiding the stigmatization attached to those who fail, i.e., the black underclass, who have constituted a new world order folk culture, which parallels the black southern folk culture of Du Bois's era, that gives rise to this continual debate regarding black double consciousness.

NOTES

1. As Francis L. Broderick (1959: 3) points out, Du Bois in his early years "learned the capitalist ethic of late nineteenth-century America: 'Wealth was the result of work and saving and the rich rightly inherited the earth. The poor, on the whole, were to be blamed. They were lazy or unfortunate, and if unfortunate their fortunes could easily be mended by thrift and sacrifice.'" Thus, in his Being-in-the-world, Du Bois, given his lack of encounter with overt discrimination (with the exception of a few racial encounters with the Irish, who were looked down upon by everyone in his community because they were poor) understands the world and the people in it through the dissolution and reformulation of his Protestant Americanism in material practice. It is in terms of this structural consciousness that he understands the racial "otherness" of the "Negroes" in the South, who, I am arguing, exercise a form of Americanism hampered by the "unfortunates" of racial discrimination. Du Bois, on the contrary, early on in his life sees their "otherness" as being part and parcel of or an aspect of their Africanness, i.e., their "doubleness," an understanding, as Adolph Reed argues he never goes back to given his later Marxist ideological leanings.

2. Du Bois, W.E.B. (1986 [1968]). *The Autobiography of W.E.B. Du Bois: A Soliloquy on Viewing My Life from the Last Decade of its First Century*. New York: International Publishers, Pp. 108.

3. Du Bois's liberal political orientation is at the center of his strife with the conservative black nineteenth-century leader, Booker T. Washington.

4. The locus of causality for Du Bois's push for communism I am not arguing is a result of the contradictory practices of his society or the system. On the contrary, my argument is that Du Bois's decision is a result of his phenomenological meditation on the nature of things. For it is feasible to have contradictory practices and yet continue the practices that give rise to the contradiction.

5. Du Bois quoted in, Hunton, Alphaeus W. (1970). "W.E.B. Du Bois: the meaning of his life," Pp. 131–137. In *Black Titan: W.E.B. Du Bois*, Edited by John Henrik Clarke et al. Boston: Beacon Press.

Chapter Four

Double Consciousness and the Liberal Black Protestant Heterosexual Bourgeois Male Identity

Du Boisian double consciousness, as demonstrated in the previous chapter, is not a reference to black American racial duality; instead, it represents the ambivalent discourse of black agents of the dominant social psychological identity, *The Liberal Black Protestant Heterosexual Bourgeois Male*, of the American social landscape seeking to exercise their discursive practice against the anti-liberal discriminatory affects of racial and class prejudice, while holding on to race and class as identity markers. W. E. B. Du Bois in *The Souls of Black Folk* autobiographically captures and articulates the consciousness and ambivalent struggles of the class, amidst racial class prejudice and discrimination, through the construct double consciousness. President Barack Obama today represents an embodiment of Du Bois's construct within an American postindustrial capitalist bourgeois world in which the discriminatory affects of racial prejudice are slowly declining amidst, paradoxically, the commodification of racial class-based identities and the ever-increasing proletarianization of the world's people of color, women, and children due to (neo) liberal bourgeois policies and ideologies. Double consciousness, be that as it may, represents the ambivalent struggle of members of the social identity, *The Liberal Black Protestant Heterosexual Bourgeois Male*, to organize and reproduce its purposive-rationality, i.e., individualism, egalitarianism, etc., amidst its contradictory practices, racial oppression, class differentiation, gender inequality, heterosexism, etc. produced by the purposive-rationality of the very ideology they seek to reproduce.

Scholars since the 1960s, the "radical" era out of which contemporary notions of African-American identity as Du Boisian "double consciousness" took shape (Allen, 1992), have described the dualism in various other ways: 1) the traditional assimilationist/nationalist readings, coming out of the humanities, which emphasize the theory as representing the "twoness" of black cultural identity; and (2) the more contemporary positivist readings which refute the latter position either on the grounds that a strict reading of the metaphor describes a form of "alienation" rather than two opposing modes of identity (Allen, 1992, 2002; Holt, 1990), or repudiate it on account of the lingering biological conception of race that persists beneath the sociohistorical attempt of Du Bois and that of the assimilationist/nationalist readings (Appiah, 1985; Reed, 1997; Crouch, 1993).

In the traditional assimilationist/nationalist readings, through which many scholars and the general public have come to interpret and understand double consciousness, the argument is that Du Bois's reference speaks to the distinct bicultural nature of black life. Hence, the historian August Meier (1959, 1963) advanced the thesis that the construct reflects Du Bois's own "ambivalent" ideological struggles (i.e., "paradox") between racial separatism and democratic rights for the "Negro" as an American. In fact, in his work *Negro Thought in America*, Meier dubbed Du Bois an "equalitarian who apparently believed in innate racial differences" (1963: 206).

Most subsequent assimilationist/nationalist interpretations of the theory share Meier's basic interpretation but view his dubious take on Du Bois's "innate racial differences" as representing the "real" and appealing choice blacks must make between two opposing cultural identities: "assimilated Americanness" or "unassimilated Negroness" (Early, 1993: xx). In other words, this position assumes, as Dickson D. Bruce's essay, "W.E.B. Du Bois and the Idea of Double Consciousness," contends,

> by double consciousness Du Bois referred most importantly to an internal conflict in the African American individual between what was 'African' and what was "American." It was in terms of this . . . sense that the figurative background to "double consciousness" gave the term its most obvious support, because for Du Bois the essence of a distinctive African consciousness was its spirituality, a spirituality based in Africa but revealed among African Americans in their folklore, their history of patient suffering, and their faith (1992: 301).

In light of these readings and critiques, some scholars, such as David Levering Lewis for example, comment that the genius of the "double consciousness" metaphor is that it transcends the assimilationist/nationalist debate or conflict by conceiving the "destiny of the race . . . as leading neither to assimilation nor separatism but to proud, enduring hyphenation" (Lewis, 1993: 281). "A biracial, bicultural state of being in the world," Bernard W. Bell posits, which signifies "a dynamic epistemological mode of critical inquiry for African Americans" (Bell, 1996: 96). A view shared by the more positivist oriented scholar, Richard L. Allen, whose sociological study, *The Concept of Self: A Study of Black Identity and Self-Esteem*, departs from Du Bois's construct (Allen, 2001: 30).

For the most part, these assimilationist/nationalist or biculturalist readings of double consciousness, assume an external validity that underscores the general contemporary understanding of the text and its prescience in capturing the dualistic nature of black consciousness. Du Boisian biographer Arnold Rampersad (1976: 74–75) comments, "[t]he 'souls' of the title is a play on words, referring to the 'twoness' of the black American," which calls "for the recognition" of their "dignity and separate identity." Eric J. Sundquist argues, "*The Souls of Black Folk* established the coherence of African American culture as a set of values and expressions that were not annihilated by slavery but nurtured by its 'voice of exile'" (1996:16).

For more nationalistic thinking scholars, the book and the construct exhibits a tension between the black Americans' national (American) and racial (black or African) identities. Reasoning along these lines, Houston Baker (1972) and Manning Marable (1986) suggest that *Souls* moves between a Victorian elitism and an appreciation for the distinct "folk culture" of the black Masses. Paul Gilroy (1993) and Bernard W. Bell (1985,1996), like many other "post-segregation-era" academics turned "public-intellectuals" (Cornel West and Henry Louis Gates also come to mind) who have appropriated "Du Bois's construct for a purely academic program" (Reed, 1997: 96), i.e., to formulate and articulate the "epistemological mode of critical inquiry" which stems from the African Americans' synthesized "double consciousness," see *Souls* as an articulation of Du Bois's own attempt to synthesize his "doubleness" (Dutch and African ancestry)—an experience which he extrapolates-from to explain African American racial and ethnic difference and their keen or critical insight (i.e., "second-sight") into "modernity" resulting from this peculiarity.

More recently, in contradistinction to these traditional readings of Du Boisian "double consciousness" "as a reference to and a confirmation of the existence of ambiguities and vacillations between assimilationist and nationalist tendencies in African American life" (Allen, 1992: 261), Ernest Allen Jr. argues that any suggestion that Du Bois's construct speaks to an internal struggle amongst the members of the tiny, educated black elite, who are "torn between the [(cultural)] values of, on the one hand, upper-or middle-class whites and, on the other, those black sharecroppers, domestics, and other working people (that is, as one might say today, between a Eurocentric and an Afrocentric cultural orientation), is, quite simply, a proposition unsupported" (Allen, 2002: 220) by a closer reading of Du Bois's own evidence in *The Souls of Black Folk*. According to Allen, the use of culture in traditional readings of Du Boisian double consciousness would be unfamiliar to Du Bois; such an interpretation is not in line with his reasoning at the time that he penned *The Souls*.

Consequently, it is this recognized (Du Bois, 1940; Meier, 1963; DeMarco, 1983; Appiah, 1985; Crouch, 1993; Reed, 1997)"neo-Lamarckian" interpretation of "double consciousness," which contains the assimilationist/ nationalist approach with the notion of an authentic "blackness," and which has dominated social science literature on understanding black racial identity and self-consciousness, then and now, I find problematic. It continues Du Bois's usage of the construct to highlight its prescience in explaining black American identity or consciousness without re-conceptualizing the metaphor and black consciousness in general given Du Bois's reliance on nineteenth-century racial sciences and national ideology to develop and articulate the theoretical and ideological metaphor double consciousness in *The Souls of Black Folk*.

Published when W.E.B. Du Bois was thirty-five and working as an economics and history teacher at Atlanta University, *The Souls of Black Folk* is a collection of nine previously published essays and five new writings. The "double consciousness" construct with which the work commenced is formulated in the essay titled "Of Our Spiritual Strivings" from Du Bois's 1897 *Atlantic* magazine essay, "Strivings of the Negro People," published in the same year as his essay, "The Conservation of Races." The significance and relevance of the construct centers on whether or not it offers a sociohistorical understanding of black American self-identity or consciousness in the context of 19th century racial science and ideology that proposed that the black race or nation was inferior to whites and had no identity, culture, souls, or consciousness aside from that acquired through their contact with "whites."

According to Kirt H. Wilson:

> [s]ix years before *The Souls of Black Folk*, in an essay titled "The Conservation of Races" (1970, original work published in 1897), Du Bois offers the following observation: "What, then, is a race? It is a vast family of human beings, generally of common blood and language, always of common history, traditions and impulses, who are both voluntarily and involuntarily striving together for the accomplishment of certain more or less vividly conceived ideals of life . . ."
>
> "physical differences of blood, color and cranial measurements" may play a part in race, but "no mere physical distinctions would really define or explain the deeper differences—the cohesiveness and continuity of these groups. The deeper differences are spiritual, psychical differences—undoubtedly based on the physical, but infinitely transcending them" (1999: 209).

These racial ideas, "physical differences of blood, color and cranial measurements", mediated by the bourgeois ideology of nationalism, Wilson further suggests, influenced Du Bois's "double consciousness" construct as the constitutive identity of black people, for in that same essay Du Bois contends:

... No Negro who has given earnest thought to the situation of his people in America has failed, at some time in life, to find himself at these cross-roads; has failed to ask himself at some time: what, after all, am I? Am I an American or am I a Negro? Can I be both? Or is it my duty to cease to be a Negro as soon as possible and be an American? If I strive as a Negro, am I not perpetuating the very cleft that threatens and separates black and white America? Is not my only possible practical aim the subduction of all that is Negro in me to the American? Does my black blood place upon me any more obligation to assert my nationality than German, or Irish, or Italian blood would (Du Bois, 1971 [1897]: 182)?

This "puzzling dilemma," brought about due to the "physical differences" of the black American as a result of race, i.e., "black blood," which grounds the "deeper differences" of their African psyche and spirituality as demonstrated in "Negro spirituals," as well as the higher ideals they shared with their former white masters, (i.e., being an American), is the basis for black "double consciousness" as the constitutive identity of the black nation. Du Bois demonstrates the construct as social reality in his autobiographical narrative *The Souls of Black Folk*.

The scientific contradictions in Du Bois's "The Conservation of Races," however, have led some theorists to refute the idea that Du Bois's "double consciousness" construct avoids the pitfalls of 19th century racial science and ideology to offer a sociohistorical understanding of black identity or consciousness. Anthony Appiah, for example, argues,

on the face of it, Du Bois' argument in 'The Conservation of Races' is that 'race' is not a scientific—that is, biological—concept. It is a sociohistorical concept. Sociohistorical races each have a 'message' for humanity—a message which derives, in some way, from God's purpose in creating races. The Negro race has still to deliver its full message, and so it is the duty of Negroes to work together—through race organizations—so that this message can be delivered (1985: 25).

But there is tension in Du Bois's alleged sociohistorical conception; "the tension," Appiah continues, "is plain enough in his references to 'common blood'; for this, dressed up with fancy craniometry, a dose of melanin, and some measure for hair curl, is what the scientific notion amounts to. If he has fully transcended the scientific notion, what is the role of this talk about 'blood'?" (1985: 25).

Thus for Appiah, Du Bois's use of "blood" is evidence that his understanding of the realities, "message," of the Negro race is grounded in the context of 19th century racial science and ideology, and therefore a failed sociohistorical attempt at understanding the "souls" or "message" of black folk.

Chapter Four

Lucius Outlaw (1996) and Bernard Boxill (1996) disagree with this strict reading of Du Bois's usage of "blood" to explain sociohistorical realities. For Outlaw, "Du Bois has not offered a definition that is intended as 'purely socio-historical.' Rather . . . he seeks to articulate a concept of race that includes both socio-historical or cultural factors (language, history, traditions, 'impulses,' ideals of life) and biological factors . . ." (Outlaw, 1996: 23). Similarly, Boxill, more philosophical than Outlaw, concludes that:

> although Du Bois allowed that cultural and historical differences tend to coincide with differences of 'blood,' he succeeded in providing a conception of race that was historical and cultural, and that he was not committed to the view that biological differences between human beings determine differences in either their histories or their cultures. Further, although his law of progress stated that the unity required for progress must be based on similarities that are given rather than merely willed, it does not make the racist claim that these similarities are similarities of 'blood,' and that people of the same color must unite simply because they are of the same color (Boxill, 1996: 65).

So, whereas Appiah sees Du Bois's usage of "blood" as his commitment to the racial science and ideology of the 19th century, Outlaw and Boxill view it as an attempt to "use the [19th century] language of race as a political project" (Bell et al, 1996:3). "A political project," according to Robert Gooding-Williams in agreement with Appiah, Du Bois inadequately carries out given his "tacit dependence on a scientific definition of 'race'" (Gooding-Williams, 1996). This dependency turns Du Bois's sociohistorical understanding of the "souls" (consciousness) of black folks into a functionalization of 19th century racial ideology or discourse as mediated by the concept of nation in order to articulate "black" national identity or consciousness in the midst of "white" consciousness (Du Bois, 1984 [1940]; Meier, 1963; Crouch, 1993; Reed, 1997; DeMarco, 1983), what Kirt H. Wilson sees as Du Bois's critical attempt toward a discursive theory of racial identity, "from a study of what race is to a study of what race means" (Wilson, 1999: 209) for black folk.

This functionalization of black racial identity or consciousness in order to define it vis-à-vis "white American consciousness" is reflected in " Of Our Spiritual Strivings" of *The Souls of Black Folk*, which provides us with the often-quoted, racialized bicultural definition of black double-consciousness that has dominated how some social scientists and scholars have come to understand black self-identity in the midst of contemporary social structural arguments, which reiterate nineteenth-century conclusions of black life in America:

> After the Egyptian and Indian, the Greek and Roman, the Teuton and Mongolian, the Negro is a sort of seventh son, born with a veil, and gifted with

second-sight in this American world, —a world which yields him no true self-consciousness, but only lets him see himself through the revelation of the other world. It is a peculiar sensation, this double-consciousness, this sense of always looking at one's self through the eyes of others, of measuring one's soul by the tape of a world that looks on in amused contempt and pity. One ever feels his twoness, —an American, a Negro; two souls, two thoughts, two unreconciled strivings; two warring ideals in one dark body, whose dogged strength alone keeps it from being torn asunder.

The history of the American Negro is the history of this strife, —this longing to attain self conscious manhood, to merge his double self into a better and truer self. In this merging he wishes neither of the older selves to be lost. He would not Africanize America, for America has too much to teach the world and Africa. He would not bleach his Negro soul in a flood of white Americanism, for he knows that Negro blood has a message for the world. He simply wishes to make it possible for a man to be both a Negro and an American, without being cursed and spit upon by his fellows, without having the doors of opportunity closed roughly in his face (Du Bois, 1995 [1903]: 43–47).

Deconstructed from its reliance on nineteenth-century racial science, this "double-consciousness" or bicultural response to refuting the inferior characterization of black consciousness and define it vis-à-vis "white American consciousness" is more a reflection of Du Bois's ambivalence about American society, an ambivalence that is grounded in his middle class Protestant liberal social identity, rather than an accurate representation of black American culture or practical consciousness.

Du Bois desires, because of his liberal bourgeois Protestantism, for himself and his race equality of opportunity, distribution, and recognition in American society, while ambivalently despising the society because of its discriminatory affects, which are grounded in the society's liberal bourgeois Protestantism, which fosters class and racial inequality. That is to say, the construct double consciousness and its contemporary usage is due in part more to the continual struggles of Du Bois's class, a particular class of black Americans, *The Liberal Black Protestant Heterosexual Bourgeois Male*, to constitute their identity amidst the contradictory practices of a racist and capitalist modernity, "class racism," which they in turn recursively organize and reproduce as liberal black bourgeois Protestantism, than to a theoretically grounded framework that characterizes the dual "practical consciousness" of the entire "African American community" comprised of liberals, conservatives, Marxists, homosexuals, feminists, Muslims, etc.

The discourse and discursive practices of this social identity, *the Liberal Black Protestant Heterosexual Bourgeois Male*, in many regards stand against the ideology of radical feminists, nationalists, Marxists, homosexuals, etc. Liberal black bourgeois Protestantism rests on two principles—on classical liberal political theory and the bourgeois Protestantism of American society, which gives rise to the "spirit of capitalism" and class inequality; it focuses on the individual black's rights and opportunities, and want to remove structural obstacles that stand in the way of individual black's entry and mobility in their occupation, profession, or the political arena, while simultaneously accepting and ignoring the economic class distinctions produced by the very logic of liberalism and bourgeois Protestantism. This is the nature Du Boisian double consciousness: liberal black bourgeois (male) Protestantism represents, since Du Bois, the dominant black social psychological identity that sought and seeks to serve as the bearer of ideological and linguistic domination for all black folk in American and world societies impacted by western culture, and double consciousness is the ambivalence members of the class experience as a result of the contradictory practices amidst, and by, which the identity is recursively organized and reproduced.

The public life of W.E.B. Du Bois and Barack Obama represent the "ideal type" models for the ambivalent struggles of this class. Du Bois, through the double consciousness construct, captures and articulates the ambivalent discourse of the social identity (i.e., the liberal, hard-working agent of the Protestant Ethic, heterosexual, black man, seeking a middle-class lifestyle for his (patriarchal) nuclear family), which he feels should characterize the discursive practice of black folks living in America once "the doors of opportunity" are opened, and Obama is the fulfillment of Du Bois's desire. Du Bois captures and articulates black identity amidst the "strife" to attain it ("self-conscious manhood") within the anti-liberal bounds of race, racial ideology, and racial and class oppression, i.e. Double consciousness represents Du Bois's personal struggle to be a liberal bourgeois male agent of the Protestant Ethic amidst the racial prejudice and discrimination of his time, which denies him the potential fruits of that identity while forcing him to see the world through a biological view of race that posits that he can not be a liberal protestant bourgeois heterosexual male because of his blackness. Hence in this reading, double consciousness is not a reference to African American biculturalism, but represents Du Bois's ambivalence about the society; his desire to be a liberal bourgeois Protestant, and derision for the society because it prevents him from doing so because of racial and class prejudice, which he reproduces, in the form of liberal black bourgeois Protestantism, in his yearning for equality of opportunity and recognition.

The life and ideals of President Barack Obama, on the contrary, is the fulfillment of Du Bois's desire. Obama is a liberal bourgeois Protestant reaping the benefits of the society, i.e., President of the United States, because the "doors of opportunity" have been opened for him and all black folks in the society. Unlike Du Bois, however, Obama exercises his liberal bourgeois Protestantism amidst "the declining significance of race" and racial ideology in a twenty-first century post-industrial landscape that is attempting to hold on to race and racial worldviews, in their commodified forms, in order to profit from them and the class inequalities produced by his liberal bourgeois Protestantism. In other words, Obama has come to traverse this twenty-first century social landscape as a *Liberal Black Protestant Heterosexual Bourgeois Male* against commodified "blacknesses," some defined along a racial reading of Du Boisian double consciousness, seeking patrons, and class oppression produced by the very consciousness he recursively organizes and reproduces. He must deny the racial reading of black consciousness given his mixed-race origins, and his success and opportunities, while holding on to the class inequality and social mobility produced by the ideals of his social psychological Protestant liberal identity. Obama has no African or Negro consciousness, but a "true [American liberal bourgeois Protestant] consciousness," revealed to him by his white mother and grandmother, which is not looked on with contempt and pity by the larger American world where class position draws more contempt than racial worldviews which have been commodified for purchase, but is labeled "elitist" and "disconnected" from the struggles and opportunities available to the black underclass of America. His life story represents the struggle to exercise his "true [American liberal bourgeois Protestant] consciousness" within an American post-industrial social context that denies the validity to racial worldviews amidst the commodification of racial identities around their class positions created by the liberal bourgeois Protestant ideas of economic gain, hard work, social mobility, etc. The black underclass, created by the dialectic of liberal bourgeois Protestant capitalism, has commodified their class position as hip-hop culture, a distinct black folk culture constituted by their musical, athletic, and hustling prowess, which are utilized as viable means to economic gain and success in the society. Obama, as a liberal bourgeois Protestant, must deny the existence of the racial and class origins of the worldview, which is paradoxically a result of his liberal bourgeois Protestantism, in order to be a liberal bourgeois Protestant.

Obama's identity and class struggle, therefore, is a twenty-first century parallel to Du Bois's own nineteenth-century struggles to be a liberal black Protestant heterosexual bourgeois male amidst the discriminatory affects of the very worldview he seeks to reproduce. Whereas Du Bois articulates his ambivalent struggle to exercise his liberal Protestantism, within an American intellectual atmosphere that emphasized racial worldviews, which denied his purposive-rationality, Obama's ambivalent struggle takes place in an intellectual social atmosphere wherein his liberal black protestant heterosexual bourgeois male identity is bounded more by his class position, which is neither African or African American but genuinely American and *soulless*, than his mix-raced background, which makes a potential patron for the plethora of black commodified racial worldviews seeking his patronage. In short, whereas Du Bois's struggle was to be recognized as a liberal *black* Protestant heterosexual bourgeois male in spite of the fact that he was black, Obama's struggle is to be recognized as a liberal Protestant heterosexual bourgeois male against any notions of blackness and the underclass positions created by his liberal bourgeois Protestantism.

Chapter Five

Barack Obama and the Demystification of Black Double Consciousness

W.E.B. Du Bois articulates his ambivalent struggles as a liberal black Protestant heterosexual bourgeois male through nineteenth-century eyes that equate identity and consciousness with race and racial ideology, forcing him to see his ambivalence, desire for equality of opportunity and recognition for blacks amidst derision for the segregation and discrimination produced as a result of the society's contempt for "poor" black life, as a sign of his biculturalism. President Barack Obama, contrarily, articulates his own ambivalent struggles in an American twenty-first century postindustrial intellectual social world where race as a determinant of consciousness and oppression has significantly declined. Albeit, the same racial prejudices surrounding black inferiority and consciousness resulting from the material conditions of "poor" black life that led to Du Bois's double consciousness response remains, however, under the guise of cultural inferiority as opposed to the racial inferiority that characterized Du Bois's era. Hence, whereas Du Bois sought to be a liberal black Protestant heterosexual bourgeois male in spite of the fact that he was black, and the majority of black folks during his lifetime were held back as a result of the liberal bourgeois Protestant identity he sought to recursively organize and reproduce; Obama, contrarily, struggles to exercise his liberal black Protestant heterosexual bourgeois male identity against being black, and "other" black racial commodified identities, which culturally clamor about the duality of black American life amidst an intellectual sociohistorical environment that argues to the contrary while celebrating commodified cultural forms constituted around class identities produced by the discursive practices of a twenty-first century liberal bourgeois Protestantism exercised within the instrumental logic of post-industrialism and consumerist globality.

This subtle difference between the origins of Du Bois and Obama's double consciousness does not negate the nature of the double consciousness construct that characterize Du Bois and Obama's dilemma as liberal black bourgeois heterosexual Protestant men; instead, it highlights the social milieu within which each social actor constituted their identity and struggle: Du Bois in a nineteenth century social milieu that views everything through racial lens, leading to an understanding of black identity grounded in mysticism, i.e., biology and spiritualism; and Obama in a twenty and twenty-first century post-racial social milieu that demystifies race, and views race and identity as products of sociohistorical processes.

This shift, in the mid-to-late twentieth-century, from biological/spiritual "races" to sociohistorical processes (culture, social structure, or the social relations of production) as the underlying factor in consciousness or identity formation did not rule out the inferiority issues associated with constructions of "blackness," which led to Du Bois's attempt in *The Souls of Black Folk* (1903) at articulating the dual and enduring racial nature of black consciousness. On the contrary, the sociohistorical turn within which Obama constitutes his identity raised some of these same issues as "many racist, liberal and Marxists social scientists argued that blacks had no real culture, that slavery destroyed it, and that what passed as black culture was simply a pathological reaction to whites, a duplication of them or an expression of lower-class culture rather than a specific black culture" (Karenga, 1993: 276). In other words, there is no "Negro-ness," "African-ness," or "blackness," associated with black American life, for these aspects of black life were destroyed during the slavery era (Frazier, 1939; 1957).

Like Du Bois, who in *The Souls of Black Folk* argued for the preservation of black Folk's dual racial nature (African and American), many social theorists then as now responded to these "racist" ideas by pointing to the survival of African culture as evidence that blacks did not completely internalize the negative images of slavery. Thus, black culture or consciousness was viewed as a synthesis of these African survivals (Africanisms) with European cultural norms, giving blacks a "double consciousness" or making them "hybrids" or "bicultural" (Allen, 2001; Asante, 1988, 1990; Billingsley, 1968, 1970, 1993; Blassingame, 1972; Early, 1993; Gilroy, 1993; Gutman, 1976; Herskovits, 1958 [1941]; Holloway, 1990a; Karenga, 1993; Levine, 1977; Lewis, 1993; Lincoln and Mamiya, 1990; Nobles, 1987; Staples, 1978; Stack, 1974; West and Gates, 1997; West, 1993).

These two contentious and controversial contemporary approaches for understanding the nature of black life or ways of being-in-the-world, i.e., consciousness, which constitute late twentieth and early twenty-first century intellectual life Maulana Karenga calls, "the pathological-pathogenic and the adaptive-vitality approaches" (1993: 280). It is within and against this intellectual framework or social milieu Obama comes to constitute and exercise his liberal bourgeois Protestant heterosexual male identity, which has given rise to his double consciousness, i.e., desire for equality of opportunity and recognition amidst derision for the society's characterization of "poor" black life paradoxically produced, as argued by theorists of the pathological-pathogenic school, by the dialectic of the very consciousness Obama seeks to recursively reproduce in order to achieve the equality of opportunity and recognition he is seeking not just for black folks, but all folks.

The pathological-pathogenic approach laid out most articulately by E. Franklin Frazier, Gunnar Myrdal, Stanley Elkins, and later Nathan Glazer and Daniel Patrick Moynihan, is predicated on the assumption that the black person is "an exaggerated American" and essentially a "pathological" reaction to whites (Elkins, 1959; Frazier, 1939,1957; Genovese, 1974; Murray, 1984; Moynihan, 1965; Myrdal, 1944; Wilson, 1978, 1987; Sowell, 1975, 1981; Stampp, 1956, 1971). Hence, "[i]n practically all its divergences, American Negro culture is not something independent of general American culture. It is a distorted development, or pathological condition, of the general American culture" (Myrdal, 1944: 928). That is, the black person "is only an American and nothing else. He has no values and culture to guard and protect" (Glazer and Moynihan, 1963: 53). Therefore, the perpetuation of families, in the black community, marked by and conducive to matriarchy, broken and ineffective males, delinquency, economic dependency, poor academic performance, and unwed motherhood are nothing more than pathologies which stem from their reaction to the brutal institutional arrangements of slavery, industrialization, and urbanization, "forces," driven by the capitalist social relations of production of the American social structure, which caused the slaves and their descendants, as E. Franklin Frazier suggests, to "take over, however, imperfectly, the folkways of the American [social] environment, discovering within the patterns of the white man's culture a purpose in life" (Gutman, 1976: 260).

The problem with this social structural approach, like Du Bois's biological determinism, is that it too is deterministic, replacing "race" and "nation" as determinants of consciousness with culture, social structure, or the capitalist social relations of production. That is, black Americans are presented as passive and "impulsive" automatons or "blank slates" programmed by their white masters with a defective (pathological) version of the structural ideology of American society (Frazier, 1966 [1939]: 32). Thus the American capitalist social structure, as recursively organized and reproduced by bourgeois whites, dominates and effaces, by threatening blacks' ontological security, anything "subjectively" African about the black American.

Du Bois in his Hegelian or dialectical parallel to the pathological-pathogenic approach—"[i]t is a peculiar sensation, this double-consciousness, this sense of always looking at one's self through the eyes of others, of measuring one's soul by the tape of a world that looks on in amused contempt and pity"—was able to maintain the distinctiveness and agency of the African, with his reliance on nineteenth-century understanding of race, i.e., biological races each have a message for the world (Du Bois, 1995 [1903]; 1972 [1897]). The structural-functional and Marxist approaches of the pathological-pathogenic school, in contrast, posits that the "other world," the American capitalist world, forced blacks to internalize its negative stereotypes (soulless, poor, immoral, uncultured, irrational, barbaric, affective and emotional) of their material conditions and "blackness," which led to black self-hatred and their attempts to live like bourgeois whites amidst their poor material conditions created by their relations to the means of production (Woodson, 1969; Frazier, 1957; Hare, 1991; Kardiner and Ovesey, 1962).

Alternatively, the adaptive-vitality approach, supplanting Du Bois's concepts of race and nation with culture, contends "that blacks could not possibly live and develop for over three hundred years simply by reacting [to and adopting 'the white man's culture']. On the contrary, blacks [, as a racial class 'for-itself,'] have made self-conscious and self constructive efforts which have contributed to American culture, not simply borrowed from it" (Karenga, 1993: 277). In this understanding, the pathologies or "divergences" of the pathological-pathogenic school are seen as African adaptive responses to the American condition, or "institutional cultural transformations" from Africa to America, which makes the culture of the descendants of slaves "neither African nor American but genuinely Afro-American," a group "identity-in-differential" to that of the American one, which cannot be compared to it (Asante, 1988, 1990; Blassingame, 1972; Gutman, 1976; Herskovits, 1958 [1941]; Levine, 1977; Sudarkasa, 1981). That is, "just as surely as black American family patterns are in part an outgrowth of the descent into slavery, so too are they partly a reflection of the archetypical African institutions and values [, i.e., affective rather than economic approach to family life, collectivity, rather than the individualism which is endemic to European culture, an egalitarian quality to relationships, an extended kin base, etc.,] that informed and influenced the behavior of the Africans who were enslaved in America" (Karenga, 1993: 282–283).

This "adaptive-vitality" response is problematic for two reasons, however. The first is related to the critique mentioned above concerning the structural determinism of the pathological-pathogenic school. That is, there is ambiguity in the concept of a *unified* African cultural inheritance, which for the most part is a biologically determined notion of blackness, structurally organizing the African's way of life against the external structural ideology of white American society.[1] Such a concept, presupposes, however, like Du Bois, a biologically, as opposed to a culturally or structurally, determined uniformity and uniqueness of African cultures institutionalized and practiced within the

American social structure, which ethnography and historical records do not completely support (Smith, 1957: 36; Holloway, 1990: 1).[2]

For example, the "adaptive-vitality" school commonly interprets the divergences of the pathological-pathogenic school to be matriarchy, "an improvisational communal consciousness," emotionalism, musical style, and intuition, elements of African culture or racial identity, which blacks have adapted to their American conditions (Gilroy, 1993; Herskovits, 1958 [1941]; Levine, 1977; Sudarkasa, 1981). The problem with this position, however, is that there are numerous cultures (Mali, Berbers, etc.) of Africa among whom these elements are not found. Moreover, there are many other peoples, including whites, among whom these practices have been reported.

This fact leads us to the second problem of the "adaptive-vitality" school, which ties it to the "pathological-pathogenic" school: assessing the impact that the structural ideology of American society, which created "blackness" as a social category for identity construction, but prevented blacks from recursively organizing or reproducing the structural or cultural terms (norms, values, proscriptions and prescriptions) associated with their heterogeneous "Africanness" or "blackness," has had on black Americans and the development of their consciousness. For by assuming the divergences of black American consciousness to be a result of their innate sense of blackness which was to some degree shielded from the institutional arrangements of slavery, the adaptive-vitality school in part overshadows and mystifies the sociocultural impact slavery had on the development of black consciousness, which in their theorizing is, "black consciousness," an element of being that is solely contingent, irrespective of the social environment, on racial (read as cultural) type. Just the same, by assuming the divergences in black consciousness to be nothing more than pathological reactions to American capitalist institutional arrangements, the pathological-pathogenic school denies the agency of black social actors.

These problems point to a serious dilemma of theorizing consciousness or identity formation; that is, how does one demonstrate agency in identity or consciousness formation without overstating the case, diluting criticism of the system or social structure for a sort of biological determinism, as in the case of the adaptive-vitality school? Likewise, the parallel dilemma is how does one emphasize the system or social structure, without contributing to the subjugation of the social actor, as in the case of the pathological-pathogenic school?

Du Bois resolves this problematic through his autobiographical construct double consciousness, which is grounded in a biological determinist worldview that attempts to explain black identity and consciousness by arguing for black racial duality amidst their struggle to achieve equality with whites. That is, black folk, for Du Bois that meant "poor" black folk, have a black worldview, which Du Bois attributes to their African spirituality or spiritualism, and a white worldview, which he attributes to his liberal bourgeois Protestantism acquired from the "Teuton" nation. For Du Bois, this fact about black identity or consciousness should not hinder blacks from achieving equality with whites if they open the doors of opportunity.

Du Bois's struggle in particular and black struggle in general "for opportunity-enhancing and outcome-based egalitarian statist policies" (Wilson, 2000: 75), however, demystified from nineteenth century biological determinism, was neither driven by the praxis of their African ways of being-in-the-world, nor a "double consciousness" /bicultural (Afro/African-American) way of being-in-the-world embedded in traditions, value-systems, ideas, and institutional forms which oppose the liberal Protestant capitalist social order of the American social structure. Rather, Du Bois's and the "black" struggle for freedom to better their material conditions, based on "opportunity-enhancing and outcome-based egalitarian statist policies," was due to the fact that the majority of "blacks," like Du Bois, who led the freedom struggle for equality of opportunity and recognition, internalized and embodied the "traditions, value-systems, ideas, and institutional forms" of the American liberal bourgeois Protestant social structure (which they reproduced as liberal bourgeois Protestantism), against fully visible, albeit ontologically insecure, "other" black "practical-consciousnesses" (African structural practices, black nationalism or pan-Africanism, conservatism, homosexuality, black communism, the pathology of the black poor, black feminism, etc.),[3] thus measuring or assessing their successes and failures, and reacting to the "other" visible black practical consciousnesses in terms of the American protestant social structure's rules of conduct, which they did and do sanction (Woodson, 1933; Frazier, 1957; Hare, 1965 [1991]; Kardiner and Ovesey, 1962 [1951]; hooks, 1981, 1994). Du Bois, in short, proposed a liberal political bourgeois ideology deduced from and "enframed" by a Protestant Ethic that focused on the individual black's rights and opportunities to achieve economic gain and a bourgeois economic lifestyle in the face of economic class and racial distinctions produced by the very logic (discriminatory affects) of his liberalism and bourgeois Protestantism.

Accordingly, it follows, it is only in relation to this "class racism" of Du Bois and members of the liberal black bourgeoisie's "form of consciousness" or practical consciousness that all other black forms of being in the American capitalist social structure become, and are, pathological-pathogenic or adaptive.[4] That is to say, it is in terms of liberal black (male) middle class push for equality of opportunity, distribution, and recognition for all blacks amidst the discriminatory affects of white class-based American society that the "double-consciousness" and the pathological-pathogenic nature of black American consciousness must be understood. Demystified, Du Bois's double consciousness is more suggestive, in the words of Frantz Fanon (1967[1952]), of the struggle, the *desire*, of members of the black (male) bourgeoisie, to prove to their former colonizers, "at all costs, the richness of their thought, the equal value of their intellect" (10)—i.e., that they can be just as human (an agent of the protestant ethic and its practice the spirit of capitalism) as the colonizers are—against their *derision* for the ontologically insecure but fully visible (albeit distorted) "other" "pathological-pathogenic" understanding of themselves, as exercised by the black poor (a class in-itself) and nationalist leaning blacks (a class for-itself), their colonizers created and discriminated against them for in order to justify closing the doors of opportunity.

Hence, this "doubleness," the *ambivalence* which arises in members of the liberal black (male) bourgeoisie when discriminated against as they struggle to prove their self-worth as liberal bourgeois agents of the Protestant ethic against negative stereotypes, images, and representations, commonly associated with nationalist leaning blacks and lower class blacks, used by whites to prevent them from achieving their aim for economic gain, equality, and recognition is the "two souls, two thoughts, two unreconciled strivings; two warring ideals in one dark body, whose dogged strength alone keeps . . . [them] from being torn asunder" (Du Bois, 1995 [1903]: 45)—as opposed to two distinct cultural epistemes for understanding the world implicit in the reliance on the biological framework—which Du Bois, in *The Souls*, autobiographically intuits as the racialized "double consciousness" of Black folk, and which the adaptive-vitality school, contemporarily, attempts to externally validate against the pathological-pathogenic understanding of black consciousness, which, from a Du Boisian perspective, is more-so a by-product of their class position as opposed to race.[5]

Like Du Bois, Barack Obama, the "mixed-race," Harvard graduate attorney and President of the United States, is a liberal bourgeois heterosexual Protestant male, who inherits Du Bois's ambivalent double consciousness struggle. Unlike Du Bois, however, Obama, inherits and inhabits a culturally commodified American intellectual social world, as opposed to a racial one, where he must fight against, or struggle between, his "true (American liberal bourgeois Protestantism) consciousness," revealed to him by his mid-western white mother and grandmother, for the need to identify with the segment of the black community that continues to hold on to a nineteenth-century definition of race to define themselves through the ideological and biological dualism inherited in Du Bois's double consciousness, and who feel that they are still held back by racial prejudice and oppression, which emanates from the very consciousness (liberal bourgeois Protestantism) Obama attempts to recursively organize and reproduce as President of the United States of America.

Obama's ambivalent struggle to be a liberal bourgeois Protestant takes place, in other words, against all mystified forms of race—because for Obama race and identity are not biologically determined, but socially constructed and fluid—while claiming to represent the struggles of all those held back by the material (class) conditions produced by his liberal bourgeois Protestantism. Hence, like Du Bois, Obama's ambivalent struggle is defined by his internal struggles regarding how best to represent and satisfy the desire for equality of opportunity and recognition of those blacks held back by racial class oppression within the metaphysical logic of the very system, liberal bourgeois Protestantism, which is holding them back, and to which Obama subscribes to and simultaneously denounce and despise. Unlike Du Bois, however, denouncing race and racial ideology for a colorblind, post-racial world "enframed" by his liberal bourgeois Protestantism constitutes his doubleness. Shelby Steele (2008) argues that this dilemma makes Obama a "bounded man," who is reluctant to make his ambivalent struggle one of race whereby he must choose between two identities (American and African-American)—for in essence Obama in his denunciation of Reverend Jeremiah Wright Jr. and ascendancy to the Presidency has chosen the sociohistorical identity that is the black Americans "true" cultural consciousness, heritage, and identity, i.e., heterosexual protestant bourgeois liberalism, against all that is African and African-American—instead he desires for all folks the promises of his liberal bourgeois Protestantism by ignoring the perversities (race and racism, sexism, classism, etc.) caused or (re) produced by his Protestant bourgeois liberalism, which continues to produce material inequality for the majority of people of color here in America and the world.

NOTES

1. My use of hegemony does not describe the African influence as an attempt to subdue and dominate the American; on the contrary, it is used to highlight the hegemonic intentions of the adaptive-vitality school's interpretation of "black culture" vis-à-vis individual black social actors.

2. This position is made famous by liberals, pan-Africanist, and nationalist leaning blacks who explain the divergences of black life by seeking to "externally validate" Du Bois's double consciousness construct in a nationalist position of their own, or as a sought of counter movement or culture to modernity (American culture).

3. This conclusion refutes both the adaptive-vitality and pathological-pathogenic schools' positions. The premise here is that "black consciousness" is not a result of an innate sense of blackness, for then all "blacks" would have one singular biologically (i.e., racially) determined consciousness. On the contrary, the practical conscious-

nesses of black folks are multiple and diverse (as a result of their (blacks) varying responses to American institutional arrangements) differentially related to, and delimited by, the dominating agential moments or responses of those (i.e., the black bourgeoisie) who have led the black struggle for freedom by recursively organizing and reproducing the agential moments of the American capitalist social structure in order to prove their self-worth within, given the society's discriminatory practices, which in that instance comes off as (given their marginalization) the contradictory practices of their society.

4. E. Franklin Frazier and the pathological-pathogenic school assess black family life in terms of the structural variables of the American social structure: the patriarchical, Protestant nuclear family. Even Du Bois (see his work *The Philadelphia Negro* 1899) in his radical understanding of black life, understands their pathological conditions in terms of his protestant structural upbringing. It is a misunderstanding to see this phenomenon as a sign of self-hatred; on the contrary, this represents attempts by agents of the protestant ethic to understand the conditions of black folk in terms of their structural paradigm. This is a practice which, as Stanford M. Lyman and Arthur J. Vidich (1985) point out, dominated early American sociological work and continues to do so as can be seen in the work of the black American sociologist William Julius Wilson.

5. Ernest Allen (1992; 2002) makes this same claim. However, his position that Du Bois's use of terms such as "double consciousness," "double ideals," and "twoness" are not in complete accord with the traditional biculturalist interpretations of the assimilationist/nationalist readings, because "the fact remains that in *The Souls of Black Folk* he neglected to use those terms in that explicit way" (1992, 262), is mistaken. For Allen's attempted "fix" and "narrow" interpretations of these terms is done at the expense of the broader context of nineteenth century (hegemonic) social scientific thought, which framed Du Bois's usage of them. That is, Allen's Frazierian (1957: 25) interpretation of Du Boisian double consciousness as the "arrested mentality of the Talented Tenth [(the black educated elites)] . . . deriving from the collapse of imputed 'double ideals' [(the socialization of the black elites in such a way as to lead them to disparage their social origins and to seek an especial kind of recognition, that is to say respect, from the dominant society—one which generally would be denied)] of this class" (1992, 269–273) fails to encapsulate the fact that the early Du Bois is suggesting that there *is* a distinct "Negroness," derived from "black blood," (i.e., African spirituality inherited in the African by their "black blood"), regardless of the Talented Tenth's achievements, which allows for their self-estrangement. Dickson D. Bruce Jr. (1992) makes this latter point—Du Bois attempts to synthesize the psychology and sociophilosophy of the nineteenth-century with its understanding of race in order to understand "black" identity formation or consciousness in the midst of "white" consciousness—clearly in his essay, "W.E.B. Du Bois and the Idea of Double Consciousness."

Bruce draws on Du Bois's possible familiarity with all the background on double consciousness from literary and medical sources to conclude that Du Bois's use of the idea of double consciousness, to characterize issues of race, emerges out of his conflating of European Romanticism and American Transcendentalism, and the field of psychology while holding on to nineteenth century racial theory (Bruce, 1992: 299–300). In the former, according to Bruce, especially in Emerson's work, the idea of "double-consciousness" refers "to a problem in the life of one seeking to take a Transcendental perspective on self and world . . . [t]he double consciousness plaguing the Transcendentalist summarized the downward pull of life in society—including the social forces inhibiting genuine self-realization—and the upward pull of communion with the divine . . ." (300). In the case of the latter (psychological sources), the term "was applied to cases of split personality . . ." (300). For Bruce,

> [a]lthough Du Bois used "double consciousness" to refer to at least three different issues—including first the real power of white stereotypes in black life and thought and second the double consciousness created by the practical racism that excluded every black American from the mainstream of society, the double consciousness of being both an American and not an American—by double consciousness Du Bois referred most importantly to an internal conflict in the African American individual between what was "African" and what was "American." It was in terms of this third sense that the figurative background [(its Transcendental and Romantic grounding)] to "double consciousness" gave the term its most obvious support, because for Du Bois the essence of a distinctive African consciousness was its spirituality, a spirituality based in Africa but revealed among African Americans in their folklore, their history of patient suffering, and their faith. In this sense, double consciousness related particularly to Du Bois's efforts to privilege the spiritual in relation to the materialistic, commercial world of white America (301).

Just the same, Bruce goes on to point out, as telling as the figurative background to double consciousness may have been, that background was supplemented in important ways by the psychological sources, which Du Bois utilized to characterize the Transcendental duality in terms of the psychological emphasis on split personality. In this sense, the spiritual nature (African) and the materialistic commercial world (American) that was the double consciousness of black folk, which like someone diagnosed with split personality, were viewed as two distinctive oppositional personalities (African and American) within a single body (304).

"Such a background of ideas and facts," as Bruce concludes, "made the concept of double consciousness especially useful to Du Bois, given his desire to develop a positive sense of racial distinctiveness out of a distinctively African heritage. Ideas of race and behavior were problematic in the late nineteenth century . . . , [for] 'Race' itself carried biological connotations—connotations not entirely absent from Du Bois's discussions—that were troublesome, since biological notions of race served mainly to ground those beliefs concerning black inferiority which were generally accepted by whites" (305).

What Du Bois attempted to do, was to portray positively, and emphasize the integrity of, blacks' distinctive nature—their African mode of thought, associated with their race, and their internalization of the American—against the inferiority understanding whites posited based simply on the African's racial type. This standpoint did not refute race but was an attempt, "[i]n the absence of any kind of adequate idea of cultural relativism," (305), to portray and articulate the experiences of Black folk, their consciousness, based on what race was as articulated in the nineteenth century (Appiah, 1985).

Chapter Six
On the Interpretation of Obama's Double Consciousness

President Barack Obama, like W.E.B. Du Bois, who coined the construct, has a double consciousness, a "twoness" grounded in the ambivalence that arises in him, and those who share his class position, as a result of his *desire* to achieve equality of opportunity and recognition in the American social structure and *derision* for that same social structure because of its discriminatory affects, classism and racism, which emanate from the dialectical contradictions of the very identity, liberal bourgeois Protestantism, he recursively organizes and reproduces in order to obtain the equality of opportunity and recognition he seeks, and in his case, eventually achieves as the first black President of The United States of America. Thus, Obama's double consciousness has nothing to do with biculturalism, being both African and American, as the traditional readings of Du Boisian double consciousness suggests, but is solely grounded in the dialectic of his Americanism as constituted by the contradictory ideologies of political liberalism and economic bourgeois Protestant (racial) capitalism, which Obama internalized and internalizes over black nationalism, conservatism, etc., growing up and socialized in a post-segregationist, post-sixties', and post-racial America in which race as a determinant of worldview and the life-chances of blacks has significantly decline amidst the ever-increasing attempt by many (poor) blacks to hold on to race as a commodified identity marker, constituted around their (underclass) class identity, against Obama's liberal bourgeois Protestantism.

It is this predominantly "racial class" basis of Obama's double consciousness that makes it distinct from Du Bois's, which is also grounded in class but is mystified by the racial ideology of the nineteenth century. Barack Obama's life-experiences and ideology in a post-segregationist, post-sixties', post-racial, post-industrial America demystifies and helps to further shed light on this ambivalent interpretation of W.E.B. Du Bois's double consciousness construct.

Barack Hussein Obama Jr. was born in Honolulu, Hawaii on August 4th, 1961. His father, Barack Hussein Obama Sr., was born and raised in a small village in Kenya, Nyangoma-Kogelo, Siaya District, where he grew up herding goats with his own father, who was a domestic servant to the British. Barack's mother, Ann Dunham, grew up in Wichita, Kansas. Her father, Stanley Armour Dunham, a furniture salesman, worked on oil rigs during the Depression, and then signed up for World War II after Pearl Harbor, where he marched across Europe in Patton's army. Her mother, Madelyn Dunham, went to work on a bomber assembly line, and after the war, they studied on the GI Bill, bought a house through the Federal Housing Program, and moved west, by way of Texas and Washington State, to Hawaii.

It was there, at the University of Hawaii, where Barack's parents met and eventually married. His mother was a student there, and his father had won a scholarship that allowed him to leave Kenya and pursue his own liberal dreams in America. After a brief marriage, Barack's parents divorced when he was two years old, and his father eventually returned to Kenya in 1963, and Barack grew up with his mother and maternal grandparents in Hawaii, and for a few years in Indonesia when his mother married Loro Soetoro of Jakarta in 1967. It is this "permanent ache of not belonging," given his "blackness" and the absence of his black African father, which is, according to Shelby Steele (2008), at the center of Obama's first book, *Dreams from My Father,* his identification with black nationalism during his college years, and his eventual choice, later on in his life, to join a "South Side black church with a 'Black Value System,' focused on 'Black freedom,' the 'black community,' and the 'black family'" at the expense of his "white" mid-western upbringing and the secularized Protestant values (i.e., the Protestant Ethic) of his maternal grandparents.[1]

Unhappy in Indonesia after his mother's second marriage (to Loro Soetoro) ended in divorce, Obama returned to Hawaii to live with his maternal grandparents. After graduating from Honolulu's Panuhou School in 1979, Obama moved to California where he attended Occidental College in Los Angeles from 1979 to 1981. Later, he moved to New York, where he graduated from Columbia University in 1983 with a degree in political science. He went on to earn his law degree from Harvard in 1991, where he became the first African American president of the *Harvard Law Review.*

Obama marries, on October 3, 1992, Michelle LaVaughn Robinson of Chicago, where Obama moved to begin his law career, at the Chicago law firm of Davis, Miner, Barnhill & Galland, and community organizing. The ceremony is officiated by Jeremiah Wright Jr., the black nationalist pastor of Trinity

United Church of Christ on 95th Street in the South Side of Chicago. Barack and Michelle have two children, Malia Ann and Natasha (called Sasha).

From 1993–2004 Obama augments his income teaching constitutional law part-time at the University of Chicago law school. He also would go on to serve more than seven years in the Illinois Senate, representing the 13th District, which covers the South Side, Hyde Park-Kenwood, and Chicago Lawn neighborhoods (Olive, 2008). After three-terms (1997–2004) as an Illinois democratic senator, a brief stance in the US senate (2004–2008), and amidst allegations of political inexperience Obama declares his candidacy for the Presidency of the United States of America in February 2007. After a long and contentious campaign against Hillary Rodham Clinton for the democratic ticket, Obama wins the nomination and goes on to overwhelmingly defeat republican candidate John McCain for the Presidency. On January 21, 2009 Barack Hussein Obama Jr. was inaugurated as the 44th President of the United States of America, making him the first "black" American president of the nation.

As the nation's supposedly first "black" American president, ironically, Obama's life-experiences and socialization neither focus on 'Black freedom,' nor take place in the 'black community,' or a 'black family'" for that matter. They are "enframed," on the one hand, by the liberal bourgeois (secular) Protestantism of his maternal grandparents; and on the other hand, by the issue of race and racial identity which clouds his biracial physical nature.[2] As such, amidst all of his accomplishments, Obama in his public life continues to struggle with, and be frustrated by, the accusations in poor African-American communities, like the South Side of Chicago, that he is "not black enough" because of his bipartisanship and ties to whites; and within white communities that he is "too black" because of his affiliation, later on in his life, with Trinity United Church of Christ and the pastor Jeremiah Wright Jr., whose black nationalist rhetoric during Obama's campaign for the presidency forced him to address the issue of race and racial identity in America.

This struggle, which Obama encounters after he leaves the multicultural state of Hawaii for college on the US mainland, with race and racial identity for the democratic liberal bourgeois Protestant "black President" is the locus of causality for his Du Boisian double consciousness. The struggle, however, does not take place in a nineteenth century modern intellectual and social milieu in which race and racial worldviews are biologically and spiritually determined constructs that are genetically determined and immutable, alas Du Bois's framework in *The Souls of Black Folk*. Quite the reverse, Obama constitutes and understands his "race" and racial identity in a post-sixties', post-racial, post-modern, and post-industrial twenty-first century intellectual and social milieu in which identity in general, and identity formation in particular, are viewed as "fluid" processes that are, and can be, multiple, diverse, and indeterminant.

In fact, in terms of race and racial identity, the intellectual and social milieu within which Obama constitutes his identity is characterized by the ideological struggles between those who, on the one hand, want to hold on to race and racial identity as a biological and immutable construct that determines worldview, i.e., the adaptive-vitality theorists, who want to hold on to the "blackness" or "Africanness" of black American identity that characterized the social and intellectual milieu of the nineteenth century; and those who, on the other hand, argue that race is not synonymous with worldview and therefore black American identity is more a product of the material experiences of blacks in the American Protestant capitalist social structure as opposed to "racial" identity, i.e., the pathological-pathogenic school. So whereas the former school views the divergences, matriarchy, extended families, Ebonics, etc., of black American life as resulting from their "Africanisms," which were retained doing the slavery process, the latter school attributes these divergences to their poor material conditions and American domestic welfare policies.

The democratic liberal black Protestant President Obama constitutes and understands, with his "fluid" concept articulated in his first book *Dreams from my Father*, the origins and nature of, his black—biracial—identity in particular, and that of the black American community in general, through the construct of the pathological-pathogenic school. Yet the struggle to identify with, and at times against, the world-view of the adaptive-vitality school, which permeates throughout inner-city communities like the South Side of Chicago, gives rise to his double consciousness, which parallels W. E. B. Du Bois's own double consciousness, i.e., the *desire* to attain self-conscious manhood along the lines of his liberal bourgeois Protestant upbringing amidst the *derision* for being associated or indexed with those who fail at the goal because of the dialectical contradictions of the very liberal bourgeois Protestant identity which suggests they can not because of their material conditions, which prior to the late twentieth-century was attributed to race.

Despite this parallel, there is a subtle difference, however, between the origins and nature of W.E.B. Du Bois's double consciousness and Obama's. Whereas, it was the case for W.E.B. Du Bois of the nineteenth century, wherein his ambivalence was a result of the fact that the majority of blacks where held back by the race prejudice of whites, whose values and ways (liberal bourgeois Protestantism) Du Bois wanted in order that he may achieve "self-conscious manhood . . . without being cursed and spit upon by his fellows, without having the doors of Opportunity closed roughly in his face (Du Bois, 1995 [1903]: 43–47) because of a contradictory racial liberal bourgeois Protestant worldview that created race as a sociobiological category, which indexed all blacks together and prevented them from participating in the liberal social structure because of their inherent inferiority from whites. For President Barack Hussein Obama, it is the reverse, his ambivalence, i.e., double consciousness, is a result of the fact that the values and ways (liberal bourgeois Protestantism) he has recursively organized and reproduced to attain self-conscious manhood, i.e., to become the first black American president of the United States of America, are looked down upon with contempt and pity not by whites, but by those black folks, the black underclass and nationalists, who lament at and point to these values and ways as the reason why they are oppressed and he is "not black enough." Seemingly, from Obama's perspective, for these black folks, closing the doors of opportunity unto themselves because they reject the values and ways they must exercise in order to achieve "self-conscious manhood" in the society. Hence their dire poverty and poor material conditions Obama seeks to redress as President, paradoxically, through his liberal bourgeois Protestantism, which alienates him from the experiences of the majority of poor and nationalistic black folks who want to hold on to race as an identity marker that makes them distinct from white folks and Obama, and who identify Du Bois and Obama's liberal bourgeois (racial) Protestantism as the source of their class positions. In short, Obama's desire is the same as Du Bois's; however, his derision is towards blacks, not whites, who close the doors of opportunity unto themselves because they reject his self-conscious manhood because it makes him "not black enough" and they view it as the source of their oppression.

This "not black enough" criticism of Obama, coming from people such as Jesse Jackson, who claim to speak for the black underclass, and his middle class liberal bourgeois Protestant orientation and position are not far-fetched. Outside of his "race," or racial phenotype, Obama's life experience, identity, and political ideology are, for the most part, conventional ones for all those who have sought the American Presidency. Obama's racial identity—which comes from his Kenyan father, who he barely knew, and growing up in a contemporary American world in which, for the most part, black Americans continue to hold on to and accept the "one drop" rule, one drop of black blood making a person black regardless of their ideological leanings, conceived in slavery—is neither distinct from his white American cultural identity he inherited from his white mother and maternal grandparents, giving him a double consciousness in the traditional readings of Du Boisian double consciousness, nor does it give him special insight into this American world that makes his liberal bourgeois Protestantism any different from any other democratic candidate to have held his position. Instead, Obama, as he demonstrably points out in his March 18, 2008 nationally televised speech denouncing the racial views of his Pastor, Jeremiah Wright, recognizes the fact that "his story" and identity is not an African American one in the bicultural sense, or any other way, but an American one:

> I am the son of a black man from Kenya and a white woman from Kansas. I was raised with the help of a white grandfather who survived a Depression to serve in Patton's army during World War II and a white grandmother who worked on a bomber assembly line at Fort Leavenworth while he was overseas. I've gone to some of the best schools in America and lived in one of the world's poorest nations. I am married to a black American who carries within her the blood of slaves and slaveowners—an inheritance we pass on to our two precious daughters. I have brothers, sisters, nieces, nephews, uncles, and cousins, of every race and every hue, scattered across three continents, and for as long as I live, I will never forget that in no other country on earth is my story even possible.
>
> It's a story that hasn't made me the most conventional candidate. But it is a story that has seared into my genetic makeup the idea that this nation is more than the sum of its parts—that out of many, we are truly one.[3]

This American singular identity, "one," which, according to Obama, is derived from the liberal yearning of the "many" seeking the so-called "American dream" through the Protestant ethic of the society, is, contrary to Obama's position regarding his candidacy, a "conventional" story for most Americans, including the black Americans many of whom their dreams were deferred as a result of *de jure* and *de facto* segregation, even though the "story is seared into [their] genetic makeup."

In fact, according to Obama, this "conventional" story is best characterized and represented by the struggles of the black American for "survival," "freedom," and "hope," as embodied in the liberal protests' of the black Protestant church—of which he was a part at Jeremiah Wright Jr.'s Trinity United Church of Christ, which embodies, not the racial, but the class experiences of "the black community in its entirety"—for equality of opportunity and recognition for black folks in America:

> In my first book, *Dreams from My Father*, I described the experience of my first service at Trinity, "[p]eople began to shout, to rise from their seats and clap and cry out, a forceful wind carrying the reverend's voice up into the rafters.... And in that single note—hope!—I heard something else; at the foot of that cross, inside the thousands of churches across the city, I imagined the stories of ordinary black people merging with the stories of David and Goliath, Moses and Pharaoh, the Christians in the lion's den, Ezekiel's field of dry bones. Those stories—of survival, and freedom, and hope—became our story, my story; the blood that had spilled was our blood, the tears our tears; until this black church, on this bright day, seemed once more a vessel carrying the story of a people into future generations and into a larger world. Our trials and triumphs became at once unique and universal, black and more than black; in chronicling our journey, the

stories and songs gave us a means to reclaim memories that we didn't need to feel shame about . . . memories with which we could start to rebuild."

That has been my experience at Trinity. Like other predominantly black churches across the country, Trinity embodies the black community in its entirety—the doctor and the welfare mom, the model student and the former gang-banger. . . . The church contains in full the kindness and cruelty, the fierce intelligence and the shocking ignorance, the struggles and successes, the love and yes, the bitterness and bias that make up the black experience in America.[4]

Thus this American liberal "one," which constitutes Obama's identity, is characterized and constituted, if we are to believe Obama in this politically driven speech, on the one hand by its liberal bourgeoisism, a desire and struggle for "survival," "freedom," and "hope" to achieve equality of opportunity and recognition for blacks given their poor material conditions produced by the very liberal bourgeoisism Obama glorifies here in his speech given in denunciation of his pastor Jeremiah Wright Jr., who in his sermons pointed to this paradox; and on the other hand, its religiosity as represented in the Protestantism, i.e., the Protestant ethic, of blacks in particular and the society in general.

As Obama tells us of this syncretized relationship between his Protestantism and the black liberal desire for equality of opportunity, distribution, and recognition for economic gain, freedom, and political rights in a speech given June 28, 2006 at the Call to Renewal's Building a Covenant for a New America conference:

It wasn't until after college, when I went to Chicago to work as a community organizer for a group of Christian churches, that I confronted my own spiritual dilemma.

I was working with churches, and the Christians who I worked with recognized themselves in me. They saw that I knew their Book and that I shared their values and sang their songs. But they sensed that a part of me that remained removed, detached, that I was an observer in their midst.

And in time, I came to realize that something was missing as well—that without a vessel for my beliefs, without a commitment to a particular community of faith, at some level I would always remain apart, and alone.

And if it weren't for the particular attributes of the historically black church, I may have accepted this fate. But as the months passed in Chicago, I found myself drawn—not just to work with the church, but to be in the church.

For one thing, I believed and still believe in the power of the African-American religious tradition to spur social change, a power made real by some of the leaders here today. Because of its past, the black church understands in an intimate way the Biblical call to feed the hungry and clothe the naked and challenge powers and principalities. And in its historical struggles for freedom and the rights of man, I was able to see faith as more than just a comfort to the weary or a hedge against death, but rather as an active, palpable agent in the world. As a source of hope.

And perhaps it was out of this intimate knowledge of hardship—the grounding of faith in struggle—that the church offered me a second insight, one that I think is important to emphasize today.

Faith doesn't mean that you don't have doubts.

You need to come to church in the first place precisely because you are first of this world, not apart from it. You need to embrace Christ precisely because you have sins to wash away—because you are human and need an ally in this difficult journey.

It was because of these newfound understandings that I was finally able to walk down the aisle of Trinity United Church of Christ on 95th Street in the South Side of Chicago one day and affirm my Christian faith. It came about as a choice, and not an epiphany. I didn't fall out in church. The questions I had didn't magically disappear. But kneeling beneath that cross on the South Side, I felt that I heard God's spirit beckoning me. I submitted myself to His will, and dedicated myself to discovering His truth.

That's a path that has been shared by millions upon millions of Americans—evangelicals, Catholics, Protestants, Jews, and Muslims alike; some since birth, others at certain turning points in their lives. It is not something they set apart from the rest of their beliefs and values. In fact, it is often what drives their beliefs and their values.[6]

It is ironic that in this speech Obama would see the social, economic, and political implications regarding an (socialist) interpretation of his Christian Protestant religiosity, i.e., "Biblical call to feed the hungry and clothe the naked and challenge powers and principalities," that diametrically opposes his, and American society's, liberal bourgeois Protestantism with its emphasis on individualism, economic gain for its own sake, and class stratification. Ironic maybe, but it is this "racial class" irony coupled with his struggle with his racial identity that is at the center of Obamaian double consciousness.

Like his Harvard counterpart W.E.B. Du Bois who also (unsuccessfully, however) ran for president, Barack Obama, who in his public life in Chicago was frustrated on the one hand with accusations in African American communities that he was not "black enough," and on the other hand in mainstream American communities that he was "too black," is a *Liberal Black Protestant Heterosexual Bourgeois Male,* who has no African consciousness but an American liberal bourgeois Protestant identity confounded by his struggle to exercise his American identity amidst the historical legacies of race, racism, and racial inequality as compounded by classism produced by the very consciousness or identity he seeks to exercise in the world. This struggle to be a liberal bourgeois heterosexual Protestant American male amidst the rhetoric coming out of white and black American communities throughout the nation that he is either "not black enough," or "too black," parallel Du Bois's own personal struggles, as a *Liberal Black Protestant Heterosexual Bourgeois Male* one hundred years earlier, against racism and classism, which gives rise to the construct double consciousness.

Du Bois, through the double consciousness construct, captures and articulates the ambivalent struggles and discourse of the social identity (i.e., the liberal, hard-working agent of the Protestant Ethic, heterosexual, black man, seeking a middle-class lifestyle for his (patriarchal) nuclear family), which he feels should characterize the discursive practice of black folks living in America once "the doors of opportunity" are opened. Obama, as a *Liberal Black Protestant Heterosexual Bourgeois Male,* is the fulfillment of Du Bois's desire and ambivalent struggle.

Du Bois captures and articulates the origins and nature of black identity amidst the "strife" to attain it ("self-conscious manhood") within the antiliberal bounds of race, racial ideology, and racial and class oppression, which prevented black folks from achieving equality of opportunity and recognition in the society. Articulated within a nineteenth century social world in which consciousness and identity formation is tied to race and biology, for Du Bois of *the Souls,* black consciousness is dual, both African and American in the bicultural sense. However, as noted before, demystified from the biological determinism of the nineteenth century, double consciousness, in this context, represents Du Bois's personal ambivalent struggle to be a liberal bourgeois male agent of the Protestant Ethic amidst the racial prejudice and discrimination of his time, which denies him the potential fruits of that identity while forcing him to see the world through a biological view of race that posits that he can not be a liberal protestant bourgeois heterosexual male because of his blackness as revealed in the practical consciousness of those blacks held back by the poor material conditions produced by the dialectic of racial Protestant capitalism in nineteenth century America. Hence in this rereading, double consciousness is not a reference to African American biculturalism, but represents Du Bois's ambivalence about the society; his *desire* to be a liberal bourgeois Protestant, and *derision* for the society because it prevents him from doing so because of racial and class prejudice, which he reproduces, in the form of liberal black bourgeois Protestantism, "The Talented Tenth," in his yearning for equality of opportunity and recognition.

The life-experiences and ideals of President Barack Obama, on the contrary, is the fulfillment of Du Bois's desire and ambivalent struggle amidst the declining significance of race in the society. Obama is a liberal bourgeois Protestant heterosexual male reaping the benefits of the society—President of the United States, because the "doors of opportunity" have been opened for him and all black folks in the society—by recursively organizing and reproducing the Protestant ethic of the society in order to achieve an "American dream" grounded in liberal bourgeois living, i.e., individualism, political rights, economic gain for its own sake, etc. Like the Du Bois of *The Souls*, he desires for all Americans, regardless of race, creed, religion, the "American dream" associated with the Protestant ethic and the spirit of capitalism despite of the class inequality (re) produced by the very liberal bourgeois living he desires and recursively organizes and reproduces. As a result, also like Du Bois, he is ambivalent about his desire because of its discriminatory affects revealed to him through the eyes of those "others" who share his "racial" identity, but feel they are held back by his "other" (white liberal bourgeois Protestant) identity; hence his double consciousness, which for Obama is more so a result of the antagonism of black America as opposed to white America as in the case of Du Bois.

So unlike Du Bois, Obama exercises his liberal bourgeois Protestantism and experiences his ambivalence amidst "the declining significance of race" and racial ideology in a twenty-first century post-industrial landscape that is attempting to hold on to race and racial worldviews, in their commodified forms, in order to profit from them and the class inequalities produced by his liberal bourgeois Protestantism. In other words, Obama has come to traverse this twenty-first century social landscape as a *Liberal Black Protestant Heterosexual Bourgeois Male* against commodified "blacknesses," some defined along a racial reading of Du Boisian double consciousness, seeking patrons, and class oppression produced by the very consciousness he (Obama) recursively organizes and reproduces. That is to say, the racial categories produced by liberal bourgeois Protestant capitalist slavery overtime relationally produced a racial caste, blacks, in class, who constituted their social identities around their "racial class" identities, i.e., the poor black underclass, whose poor material conditions gave rise to a pathological-pathogenic way of life that was as such because of its relation to the bourgeois Protestantism of a group of black pastors and professionals, E. Franklin Frazier's black bourgeoisie, who desired to live and be recognized by whites, but were indexed with all blacks regardless of their class positions.

Whereas race and racial ideology of the nineteenth and early twentieth century reified the worldviews of the earlier classes in the black community; contemporarily, commodification in post-industrial capitalist America serves the same purpose that race did two centuries earlier. In the nineteenth century biology was the locus of causality for black consciousness or identity. Today, the commodification of the class positions in black America has reified black consciousness around both the liberal/conservative bourgeois Protestant identities or practical consciousnesses of the middle and upper classes, and the nationalistic/hip hop cultural identity of the black underclass.[7] Blacks are either middle/upper middle class or underclass based on the type of clothes they purchase to wear, music they listen to, schools they attend, cars that they drive, etc., as opposed to their biology or "blackness." Hence, whereas Du Bois had to hold on to race as a worldview, because of its biological and spiritual origins, in order to articulate his double consciousness, mystifying double consciousness under the umbrella of biological determinism, biculturalism, and spiritualism. Obama must deny the racial reading of black consciousness given his mixed-race origins, his success and opportunities, and his post-industrial "fluid" understanding of race and racial identity, while recognizing and struggling with the class inequality and social mobility produced by the ideals of his social psychological Protestant liberal bourgeois identity, which is revealed to him through the worldviews of those blacks in dire poverty and poor material conditions throughout urban America where hip-hop culture as a supposedly African American commodified cultural form is juxtaposed against the liberal bourgeois Protestantism of middle and upper-middle class black America.

Hence, Obama has no African or Negro consciousness, but a "true [American liberal bourgeois Protestant] consciousness," revealed to him by his white mother and grandmother, which is not looked on with contempt and pity by the larger American world where class position draws more contempt than racial worldviews which have been commodified for purchase, but is labeled "elitist" and "disconnected" from the struggles and opportunities available to the black underclass (and poor whites) of America whose commodified worldview, hip-hop culture, is juxtaposed against liberal bourgeois Protestantism as the only authentic black worldview, and the latter identity that of whites. Obama's life story, and his double consciousness, represents the struggle to exercise his "true [American liberal bourgeois Protestant] consciousness" within an American post-industrial social context that denies the validity to racial worldviews and groups amidst the commodification of racial identities around their class positions created by the liberal bourgeois Protestant ideas of individual liberty, economic gain, hard work, social mobility, class stratification, etc. The black underclass, created by the dialectic of liberal bourgeois Protestant capitalism, has commodified their class position as hip-hop culture, a distinct black folk culture constituted by their musical, athletic, and hustling prowess, which are utilized as viable means to economic gain and success in the society over the education, hard work, and delayed gratification posited by liberal black Protestant heterosexual bourgeois males. Obama, as a liberal bourgeois Protestant, must deny the existence of the racial and class origins of the worldview, hip-hop culture, which is paradoxically a result of his liberal bourgeois Protestantism, in order to be a liberal bourgeois Protestant, the same worldview Obama sees as key to "reclaiming the American dream" for all of

America. This alienates him from the black underclass, because seemingly he exercises a worldview that is" not black [(enough)]," but white, and associated with oppression and exploitation.

Obama's identity and class struggle, therefore, is a twenty-first century parallel to Du Bois's own nineteenth-century struggles to be a liberal black Protestant heterosexual bourgeois male amidst the discriminatory affects of the very worldview he seeks to reproduce. Whereas Du Bois articulates his ambivalent struggle to exercise his liberal Protestantism, within an American intellectual atmosphere that emphasized racial worldviews, which denied his purposive-rationality, Obama's ambivalent struggle takes place in an intellectual social atmosphere wherein his liberal black protestant heterosexual bourgeois male identity is bounded more by his class position, which is neither African nor African American but genuinely American and *soulless*, than his mix-raced background, which makes him a potential patron for the plethora of black commodified racial worldviews seeking his patronage while looking on in amused contempt and pity at his liberal bourgeois Protestantism. In short, whereas Du Bois's struggle was to be recognized as a liberal *black* Protestant heterosexual bourgeois male in spite of the fact that he was black, Obama's struggle is to be recognized as a liberal Protestant heterosexual bourgeois male against being black and elitist. That is, against any notions of blackness and the underclass positions, created by his liberal bourgeois Protestantism, which look on in amused contempt and pity at his social identity because it is that of whites, and, by logical deduction, oppressive, exploitative, and "not black enough."

Interestingly enough, for Obama the answer to this dilemma of being American against being African American and the sociopolitical economic problems facing not just black America, but the "one" America to which he claims to belong, is not less liberal bourgeois Protestantism, following the "trickle down" economics (Reaganomics) of former President Ronald Reagan, in favor of a black nationalistic/socialistic program to help poor black folks. Instead, his answer to his dilemma and the problems facing a post-George W. Bush era is more liberal bourgeois Protestantism for all (middle and working class) those prevented from achieving the "American Dream." Obama's second book, *Audacity of Hope: Thoughts on Reclaiming the American Dream* (2006), and his stimulus package, are just that, compilations of liberal bourgeois Protestant bipartisan policy prescriptions (Reaganomics for the middle classes) for aiding middle and working class families to achieving the "American dream" in spite of the continuing social class stratification dialectically reproduced by his and the society's liberal bourgeois Protestantism with its emphasis on growth resulting from job creation, hard work, and economic gain.

Du Bois towards the end of his life rejected this liberal bourgeois Protestant worldview for communist pan-Africanism, which was conceived out of the dialectical contradictions between the ideals of liberal bourgeois Protestantism and the material contradictions of its praxis. Obama, like the neoconservatives of the George W. Bush Presidency, however, has sought a return to a soulless liberal bourgeois Protestantism that threatens all life on earth via the continual ever-increasing proletarianization of the world's people of color and ecological devastation and destruction due to capitalist overproduction and exploitation, i.e., its continual material contradictions.

To this end, Obama's identity and aims parallels the barbaric identities and aims of the invading barbarian hordes of the Roman Empire who sought to identify with and reproduce a "hybrid" Roman way of life amidst the political, economical, and social decline of Roman civilization. Consequently, either President Obama will continue the liberal bourgeois Protestant course of his white predecessors thereby sealing the fate of the American republic in the dialectic of its liberal Protestant bourgeois discourse, with its emphasis on wealth and overproduction amidst class inequality and ecological devastation, or he will follow the words of W.E.B. Du Bois to Africa prior to his death and:

> Refuse to be cajoled or to change your way of life so as to make a few of your fellows rich at the expense of a mass of workers growing poor and sick, and remaining without schools so that a few black men can have automobiles.
>
> Africa here is a real danger which you must avoid or return to the slavery from which you are emerging.

NOTES

1. Steele, Shelby (2008). "A Bound Man: Why we are Excited about Obama and Why He can't Win." New York: Free Press, pg. 53.

2. I use the term "secular" here to denote the ever-increasing rationalization of the Protestant Ethic, which to Obama's maternal grandparents are not religious values but part of the American non-religious value-system or creed, which Obama would come to value.

3. Barack Obama cited in Olive, David (2008). "An American Story: the Speeches of Barack Obama. Canada: ECW Press, pg. 256.

4. Barack Obama cited in Olive, David (2008). "An American Story: the Speeches of Barack Obama. Canada: ECW Press, pg. 259.

5. Jeremiah Wright's sermons speak to the fact that American foreign policy and treatment of blacks are directly related to its economic liberal and racist ideology, a fact Obama must deny or distance himself from in order to paint himself as the ideal liberal bourgeois Protestant democratic candidate for the American presidency.

6. Barack Obama cited in Olive, David (2008). "An American Story: the Speeches of Barack Obama. Canada: ECW Press, pg. 170–171.

7. The difference between the bourgeois Protestantism of conservatives, such as Shelby Steele, Ward Connerly, Clarence Thomas, for examples, and Obama and Du Bois's liberal bourgeois Protestantism is that the former do not have a double consciousness. That is, they do not attribute the failure of those blacks trapped in dire poverty to race or the dialectic of their bourgeois Protestant social structure. Instead, for conservative bourgeois blacks the locus of causality for black failure is attributed to individual effort or lack thereof and victimization.

Chapter Seven

Black Consciousness Today and the *Liberal Black Protestant Heterosexual Bourgeois Male* Identity

In the course of this work I have attempted to examine the nature of black practical consciousness in general, and Barack Obama's social identity or practical consciousness in particular, and their relation to W.E.B. Du Bois's double consciousness construct. The underlying assumption has been that Du Bois's construct black double consciousness should be understood in relation to the purposive rationality (i.e., the imaginary "fictive ethnicity," or "class racism," (Etienne Balibar's terms)) of the liberal black Protestant heterosexual bourgeois male social class identity represented best in the personhoods' of W.E.B. Du Bois and Barack Obama. The purposive-rationality of members of the class, and the aforementioned social actors, since the Civil War, has been for equality of opportunity, distribution, and recognition with their white counterparts, rather than representing a real community, or nation, defined by its "doubleness" or dual ethnicity. Double consciousness represents the *Liberal Black Protestant Heterosexual Bourgeois Male*'s ambivalent struggle to exercise their American liberal bourgeois Protestant practical consciousness with its emphasis on equal rights, economic gain, and integration, amidst their derision for the discriminatory affects, embodied in the class position of members of the black underclass whose class positions are a result, of the very identity they, Du Bois and Obama for example, recursively organize and reproduce in order to be in the American social structure.

In positing this ambivalent reinterpretation of Du Boisian double consciousness from its traditional bicultural reading, an important starting point was to trace the history of black American consciousness or identity development in slavery. Slavery had a profound impact on the political, social, economic, and social psychological life of the African slaves who came in the main from West Africa where diverse cultural practices existed from polygamous matriarchal societies to Islamic cultural practices. While scholars of the pathological-pathogenic school have viewed the brutal social psychological impact of slavery on these differences as obstacles to the development of an authentic black culture or social cohesion thereby pointing to the fact that the divergences of black life in America are a result of their poor material relations to the means of production of the social structure, scholars of the adaptive-vitality school have pointed to the retentions of Africanisms in ways of thinking, behaving, and speaking.

Subsuming the black American historical experience within a structurationist understanding of the liberal bourgeois Protestant constitution of American society and its social psychological identity or practical consciousness, I rejected the position of both schools. I demonstrated instead that black practical consciousness within the American liberal bourgeois Protestant social structure as administered and determined by the white Protestant heterosexual male elites of the nation-state became multiple and diverse, but dominated by the practical consciousness of the liberal black Protestant heterosexual (male) bourgeoisie or middle class which for a long time served as the bearers of ideological domination in American society in their quest for political, social, and economic integration against all other adaptive-vital black American identities or consciousnesses, which were incorporated into, and assessed in relation to, the practical consciousness of the liberal black Protestant heterosexual bourgeois male social class identity.

Specifically, I reinterpreted the historiography of how the institution of slavery impacted and re-shaped African practical consciousnesses within the American liberal bourgeois Protestant social structure embodied in, and administered by, the American nation-state. Black Africans were introduced into the American Protestant liberal bourgeois capitalist social structure as black slaves. American whites through the laws of the land, i.e., slave codes, miscegenation laws, social norms and practices represented their African practical consciousnesses as primitive forms of being-in-the-world to that of the dominant American white Protestant bourgeois social order (Patterson, 1982: 38).

From this relational perspective, and in keeping with the dominant structural interpretation of the pathological-pathogenic school, I illustrated the structural forces—race, class, and status—under the slavery mode of production of the American capitalist liberal bourgeois Protestant social order that eventually, under the "contradictory principles of marginality and integration" (Patterson, 1982: 46), shaped the majority of African consciousness as a "racial class-in-itself" (blacks), a "caste in class," forced to embody, for their ontological security, the structural terms (good, obedient, pious, religious slaves) of the dominant American (capitalist) social relations of production over all other "alternative" African adaptive responses, maroon communities, black conservatism, Muslims, etc., to its then organizational form, or mode of production, slavery. This embodiment of bourgeois ideals, in the guise of the protestant work ethic of good pious slaves, by the majority of Africans amidst their poor material conditions relationally stood against "other" black or African American social psychological identities, black conservatism, black nationalism, black feminism, which I conclude, eventually converted black American identity amongst a few blacks into a black bourgeois Protestant type whose sole aim, under the leadership of black men like W.E.B. Du Bois, in the general American social structure was for equality of opportunity, distribution, and recognition with whites. This made the struggle for freedom amongst these blacks nothing more than a black middle class heterosexual male phenomenon as the more "liberal" arm of the best of the house servants, artisans, and free blacks from the North, acting as a structurally differentiated "racial class-for-itself," a "caste in class," sought to define the black situation for all blacks, in terms of the society's bourgeois ideals (temperance, economic gain for its own sake, and good moral character), which they acquired through "ideological apparatuses" defined by their white Protestant male capitalist masters who viewed black emotionalism, intuition, disobedience, "immorality," and "barbarity" as contrary to white civilized liberal bourgeois Protestantism. It is, I argued, the ambivalence of the liberal black (male) bourgeoisie or middle class, their *desire* to obtain equality of distribution and recognition amidst their *derision* and contempt for the racial discrimination they face, as a "racial caste-in-class" in the American social structure that W.E.B. Du Bois (as a member of this class) captures with his double consciousness construct.

Thus, as I further demonstrated, through an analysis of W.E.B. Du Bois's *habitus* or "practical consciousness," the embodiment of liberal black bourgeois Protestant middle class interest, the dominant agential moments of the American social structure, amidst the racial discrimination faced by blacks as they sought and seek to exercise these interests in order to better their material conditions and obtain equality of opportunity, distribution, and recognition with their white American counterparts, is the sole reason for this double consciousness or biculturation highlighted by Du Bois, which Barack Obama embodies contemporarily, against the discriminatory affects of the black underclass whose class position is a result of the liberal bourgeois Protestant social psychology identity he and Obama embody and attempt to recursively organize and reproduce.

This reinterpretation of Du Boisian and Obamaian double consciousness as the internal ambivalent dilemma that arises from their social psychological class identity, liberal black heterosexual bourgeois male Protestantism, amidst the discriminatory affect of that identity, negates the adaptive-vitality school's attempt to rely on Du Bois's concept to externally validate the duality or biculturalism of black American consciousness. Although Du Bois's double consciousness construct may have started off as the notion that black consciousness is divided between two distinct epistemologies and ontologies, given his reliance on nineteenth century racial and national ideology to understand black "practical consciousness" amidst that of white protestant America, my sociohistorical understanding and deconstruction of the construct reveals it to be more of a description of ambivalence, amongst the liberal black bourgeoisie or middle and upper middle class blacks, rather than a distinct ethos from that of the protestant ethic and spirit of capitalism by which many black Americans (with bourgeois upper middle class sensibilities) recursively organize and reproduce their material resource framework.

In short, I conclude that the construct is the embodiment of Du Bois's, as a representative of the liberal black bourgeoisie, "class racism;" Du Bois, through the prism of liberal black Protestant heterosexual male nationalism, desires, for his predominantly "poor" race and nation, the bourgeois ideals of the American capitalist social structure in order to reject the contempt to which blacks as second class citizens are subject as a result of the very consciousness he yearns for. He advocates, in the face of class and racial discrimination, for the "educated" elites ("The Talented Tenth") of the black nation ("pan-Africanism") throughout the world to establish "Negro" institutions "for the purpose of raising such peoples to intelligence, self-knowledge and self-control" so that they can be recognized in the kingdom of cultures, i.e., obtain equality of opportunity, distribution, and recognition with their white counterparts. Du Bois, after 1903, dismissed this liberal ideological and practical orientation for pan-African communism, which denounced the class basis and social structure of inequality in American liberal bourgeois Protestant society.

Like the Du Bois of *the Souls*, Barack Obama subscribes to this early liberal bourgeois Protestant ideology of Du Bois over his (Du Bois's) later pan-African communist orientation. Unlike Du Bois, however, Obama's ambivalence, and subsequent double consciousness, is no longer a result of white racism, but stems from the antagonism of a segment of black America whose underclass position and social psychological identity, created by the material dialectic of Obama's liberal bourgeois Protestantism, is glorified and celebrated as an authentic black ethos over Obama's liberal bourgeois Protestantism which is looked upon with contempt and pity by the black underclass and those who claim to speak for the identity. In essence, Obama has claimed liberal bourgeois Protestantism over Du Bois's democratic communism, black conservatism, and the racial politics of those (the black underclass) who are held back by the dialectic of Obama's liberal bourgeois Protestantism. His double consciousness results from the fact that his class position is looked upon with contempt and pity by the black underclass and their spokespersons who point to it as the locus of causality for their dire poverty and underclass position, which Obama, as President of the United States seeks to ameliorate through his liberal bourgeois Protestant ideology as encapsulated in his incessant call for a reaffirmation of "the American Dream."

Whether the liberal bourgeois Protestantism of the liberal black Protestant bourgeois heterosexual male, as embodied in Du Bois and President Obama, or the so-called authentic black cultural consciousness of those, the black American underclass whose culture is embodied in hip-hop culture, held back in dire poverty by the material dialectic of the latter, Black Americans today under consumer capitalism have gone a long way from living up to the image of their puritan masters—thrift, frugality, and relentless self-denial can hardly be considered at the present time to be their outstanding characteristics. Yet the essence of "the Protestant Ethic and the spirit of racial capitalism" and the ambivalence, which characterized the early Du Bois and Obama's own consciousnesses are still the basis for the group's practical consciousness and problematic under late twentieth and early twenty-first century post-industrial (consumerist) capitalist organization.

Dominated and led by a segment of their population, the liberal black Protestant heterosexual male bourgeoisie—who's adaptive-vitality to enslavement was incorporation of the structural terms, i.e., class and status, of the American social structure—with a middle class sensibility and concerned with civil rights, assimilation, and "positive" black images, their (the liberal black Protestant heterosexual male bourgeoisie) continual gaze "back upon the eye of power" to allow them to partake in the order of things, comes from, and is driven by, their reproduction of the reified consciousness of the rational American capitalist liberal state amidst the material contradictions produced by the very identity, liberal bourgeois Protestantism, they seek to recursively organize and reproduce in their material practice. The American nation-state through its ideological apparatuses, i.e., the law, public education, churches, the organization of the family, interpellates and "embourgeois" these black subjects with their wants, needs, and ideals (consciousness), which they subscribe to and ideologically reproduce in their own Negro Academies—black colleges, churches, fraternities and sororities, etc, in order "to attain self conscious manhood" and reject the contempt to which they were and are subject—in spite of the fact that the material contradictions inherent in their liberal bourgeois Protestant ideology was and is the locus of causality for the material conditions and ideals, of those in poverty, for which they were and are held in contempt for.

The struggle of this segment (the liberal black Protestant heterosexual male bourgeoisie) of black America, prior to (when they numbered 5 percent of the black population), and since (25 percent), Du Bois, has been for equality of opportunity (for distribution and recognition), because that is what has been lacking in their relation with whites, not to recognize or exercise a distinct ethos, which never materialized amongst the majority of the masses given that power delimited the social structure they had to be in by marginalizing ("class racism") their very being, i.e., African ethos, in relation to the liberal bourgeois Protestantism of heterosexual white males. The African, a deployable unit of the American social structure, sought to be an agent of the social structure by having to disprove, warred against through the exercise of the praxis of the social structure, like their white counterparts, the ideas and practices of the poor "other's" held back by the material contradictions of their identity, by which they were marginalized.

Amongst the liberal black Protestant heterosexual male bourgeoisie the end product was a "colored" American whose only subversive act, given the need to disprove the contempt to which they were and are subject as revealed in the material conditions and practices of the black poor, was and is to recursively organize and reproduce the "pure" identity of authority to its "purest form" in order to obtain equality of opportunity, distribution, recognition with their white counterparts in spite of the material contradictions produced by the material practices of the society's social identity, which is revealed in the material conditions of the black underclass (Frazier, 1957; Hare, 1965 [1991]; Woodson, 1933 [1969]).[1]

On an individual level, Obama's rise to the American presidency is an ideal illustration of this aim and direction black identity or practical consciousness has assumed after almost 400 years in the country over Du Bois's later insistence that they reject it in order to turn their gaze unto themselves and resolve the material contradictions of those "poor" blacks held back by the dialectic of liberal bourgeois Protestantism.

As a group, during the Black power era (1965–1979) there was an attempt by the Black Panthers to do just as Du Bois suggested and turn their gaze inward and establish Negro academies that grappled with the needs of a "poor" people as opposed to reproducing in their material practices a soulless (ideological-mechanical) reified-consciousness presented as the nature of life as such (the liberal bourgeois Protestant middle class response) that was responsible for their dire poverty and material conditions. This, however, came to pass as J. Edgar Hoover and his "counterintelligence program" sought to "expose, disrupt, misdirect, discredit, or otherwise neutralize the activities of black nationalist, hate-type organizations and groups, their leadership, spokesmen, membership, and supporters, and to counter their propensity for violence and civil disorder" (Hoover, 1997 [1967]: 134).

What was produced in turn, from the 1970s onwards, was the continual disjuncture, which dates back from slavery, between the ideologies of those looking to turn their gaze inward (i.e., black nationalist, pan Africanist, communist groups, and religious groups such as the Nation of Islam) and those gazing back upon the eye of power (i.e., the liberal and conservative black Protestant bourgeoisie) for opportunity and recognition. The latter, as was the case during slavery, prevailed, and their continual protest for economic gain and recognition is rationalized and represented in the reified consciousness of the society as the proper way of doing things—which in turn is taught in the society's "ideological apparatuses" using representatives who have succeeded (liberal black Protestant bourgeoisie) that way as examples for the rest of the discriminated against (black underclass, pan-Africanists, nationalists, homosexuals, communists, etc.)—despite of the fact that the disjuncture between the two positions is a result of the material contradictions inherent in the liberal bourgeois Protestant thought and practices of liberal and conservative bourgeois Protestant blacks. This integrationist aim for all of black America was the driving force behind W.E.B. Du Bois's *The Souls of Black Folk*, and it is the drive behind Tavis Smiley's new work, *The Covenant with Black America* (2006) and Barack Obama's *Audacity of Hope* (2008), which seeks to lay a liberal black middle class plan of action for black America to integrate more into the fabric of American capitalism amidst the continual contempt to which they are subject as a result of the ever-increasing proletarianization and criminalization of the black masses whose material conditions are due to the very liberal bourgeois Protestantism subscribed to and prescribed by Du Bois, Smiley, and Obama.

Thus, contemporarily, the historical evolution of the practices of members of the liberal black Protestant heterosexual bourgeoisie, who have led the integrationist movement for black America, has resulted in the legitimation of the Protestant and capitalist practices of the American social structure as the nature of reality and existence as such, and the nature (i.e., structural terms—class and status) by which all (blacks) must assess and reproduce their being-in-the-world in spite, or despite, of the material contradictions, poverty, political impotence, etc., produced among the (black) poor due to the material contradictions of the very identity the group seeks to organize and reproduce in order to achieve equality with whites.

This acceptance of the structural (class) terms of the society in order to ameliorate racial stigmatization has led to the "declining significance of race" as black participation or integration in the social structure has resulted in their continual class stratification in which a dwindling middle class living in suburbs is assimilated and isolated from a poor "underclass," living in urban inner-cities, who do not have a distinct practical consciousness from that of the black middle class as suggested by conservative integrationists such as Thomas Sowell (1975, 1981) and Shelby Steele (1990); on the contrary, their conspicuous consumptive practices and so-called cultural identity, hip-hop culture, in post-industrial capitalist America are a pathological-pathogenic reflection of the structural terms of the society constrained by the poor material conditions of their structured resource framework (Gutiérrez, 2004; Geronimus and Thompson, 2004; Mocombe, 2004).

In other words, the black underclass, structurally differentiated permanent poor "others" i.e., discriminated against minority, due to low level of education and few marketable skills in an urban environment in which work has disappeared to developing countries, they, black underclass, are segregated from a scattered black bourgeoisie who ape after the "American dream" via education and professional training. Isolated from both white and black middle class professional America, they (i.e., the black underclass) are an entrapped population of poor persons, used, unwanted, and unemployed, welfare dependents who, given their ideological indoctrination by institutional regulators of the media, schools, and other ideological apparatuses, also ape after the American dream (Wilson, 1978; 1981; Massey and Denton, 1993). Subsequently, lately that is, they have developed a commodified way of life among themselves (hip-hop culture) centered on the means that are most likely in their poor urban environments to provide opportunity, recognition, and "economic gain" i.e., music, athletics, drugs, prostitution, pimping etc., amidst their "hardship in poverty," "poor land and low wages," "race prejudice and legal bonds," and "ignorance and dire poverty."

This commodified way of life in post-industrial capitalist America has become the global youth culture of the twenty-first century. It (hip-hop culture) is a distinctively American cultural phenomenon, which stems from the segregating and differentiating class processes of "the spirit of capitalism." Many black power elites (black bourgeoisie) who have led and continue to lead the integration movement (gazing back to power for recognition) either attempt to clean up elements of "Hip-Hop culture," as a distinct black culture rooted in African spiritual and musical ideals, in order to market and profit from it (Russell Simmons, etc.); or they (Jesse Jackson, Al Sharpton, Bill Cosby, Winston Marsalis, Glenn Loury, Shelbe Steele, Stanley Crouch, members of the Congressional Black Caucus, etc.) shun it, through either a conservative or liberal prism of a Protestant and moralizing ethos, hypocritically disapproving of its promiscuous, nihilistic, masochistic, and homophobic language and form of being in the world—in most cases in favor of Jazz and a moral ethic grounded in the Protestantism of Du Bois's era—which some argue can be transformed either through structural forces (i.e., Affirmative Action and the welfare state) or a form of behaviorism that emphasizes self-love, (nuclear) patriarchal family, education, professional calling, and community, i.e., an "embeddedness" of the Protestant ethic and the spirit of capitalism.

In either case, the liberal model which emphasizes structural solutions or the conservative model which emphasize self-help, my point is that this is no ground to argue for a bicultural reading of Du Bois's double consciousness; it simply points to the continual struggle of how best to (re) present the racial images of the black, dark-skinned, American—whites seem to prefer the black professional class—within the agential moments (structural variables, i.e., class and status) of racial class gendered Protestantism and its differentiating structural practice, the spirit of capitalism: the black underclass or the professional class.

This contemporary "racial class" ambivalent struggle amongst post-segregationist black American scholars and professionals, like Smiley and Obama, I see as the parallel to W.E.B. Du Bois's own early ambivalent struggle to disassociate himself from negative images, due to "hardship in poverty," "poor land and low wages," "race prejudice and legal bonds," and "ignorance and dire poverty," in order to partake in the "class" fabric of American sociopolitical life. In fact, it is the basis for the insistent clamor for this notion of a black double consciousness today (albeit race and nation are now supplanted by African cultural elements) as each generation of blacks, alas Barack Obama, strives to partake in the order of things, while attempting to avoid failing and being stigmatized with the entrapped sector of the population, the black underclass, who looks like them, and who paradoxically fail because of the Protestant capitalist social structure by which they reproduce their lives that is represented in dialectical opposition to the practices of bourgeois Protestant liberal and conservative living (Watkins, 1998; Mason, 1996; Reed, 1997).

This reading is not intended to discredit the dynamics involved in blacks trying to establish a distinct ethos; but to suggest that this takes place within a singular hegemonic ideological mechanical solidarity, a reified consciousness, dominated, contemporarily, by two classes, the black middle class and "underclass" agents of the protestant ethic, who position themselves as the bearers of ideological domination for black folk and bar those (Nation of Islam, black communists, feminists, homosexuals, etc.) who misinterpret their signifiers or choose another form of being-in-the-world from partaking in the order of things.[2] Paradoxically, given the fact that the latter group (black underclass) is segregated and entrapped, one would think, alas Karl Marx's dialectic, in light of their poor material conditions, that it is among them that a distinct anti-structural black ethos should have developed, against the liberal and conservative bourgeois Protestantism of their middle class brethrens, but in fact they identify with the ethos of the larger society—through the black middle class and whites who direct the churches and educational ideological apparatuses in their segregated communities as pastors, principals, and teachers—and ape for American materialism "by any means necessary," i.e., sports, music, drugs, crime, etc. A striving driven by the soulless aim of an American liberal bourgeois Protestant capitalism, which they (black underclass) so desperately attempt to recursively reproduce in their poor material conditions, "to make a few . . . fellows rich at the expense of a mass of workers growing poor and sick, and remaining without schools so that a few [(predestined)] black men can have automobiles" (Du Bois, 1970).[3]

This is the soul-less, immoral, aim that black practical consciousness has taken after almost 400 years in a soul-less social structure of inequality that seeks to hegemonically dominate the world, exhaust its natural resources, and destroy the environment and humanity because of its overproduction and incessant need for economic gain. Ideologically concealed under the veneers of a religious Protestantism taught in many mega-churches, many black folks' Protestant Ethic and the spirit of capitalism does not allow them to question or protest against the predatory effects of a liberal bourgeois Protestant global capitalism, which is enslaving the world's people of color for the economic gains of the middle class and their slavemasters, the upper-class of owners and high-level executives. Instead, "the blessings of riches," as a sign of their salvation, is preached every Sunday, and their lives become centered on the accumulation of goods and capital for economic gain and conspicuous consumption, this in spite of the fact that the rise of the black bourgeois middle class, like their white counterparts, is, ironically, at the expense of the world's people of color. Instead of refusing to be cajoled to participate in a world which seeks to make a few of their fellows rich at the expense of the mass of workers of color of the world growing poor and sick, and remaining without schools, many black folks, like their white counterparts, recursively organize and reproduce their "soul-less" Protestant ethic and the spirit of capitalism so that a few black men can have "bling" "bling" as a sign of their salvation and predestination in the face of poverty related deaths throughout the world and urban America.

How can black folk truly serve as the "moral consciousness" of America as articulated by liberal blacks such as Tavis Smiley, Barack Obama, Eric Dyson, etc., amidst the pervasiveness of black on black crime, and the preaching of a religiosity contingent upon material wealth for a few as a sign of their blessing and salvation? To truly be associated with the righteous nations of the 25th chapter of Matthew in the Holy Bible, and be the moral consciousness of the American nation, the souls' of black folk must be constituted and recognized not by the recognition of its "African-Americanness," but by its "doubleness," which rejects it liberal bourgeois Protestantism for their worldly attempt to resolve the dialectical material contradictions of that worldview. That is, their worldly attempt to feed the hungry, give drink to the thirsty, shelter the stranger, clothe the naked, visit the sick, and come to the aid of those in prison in a soul-less society that creates the converse of these practices for the sole purpose of proving its predestination via economic gain and military might at the expense of the masses of black America and the world's people of color growing poor and sick.

NOTES

1. Even if one were to make the argument, as I take Bhabha to be doing, that hybridity is a necessary result of the interaction between power and the discriminated against; it does not hold that hybridity exists as a subversive force if the discriminated against accepts the terms of those who discriminate against them, which is my argument. Bhabha's emphasis focuses too much on the physical body, devoid of distinct practices, as the site for subversion.
2. There are many blacks in academia who have rejected the normative order of things for an afrocentric worldview and communism. However, being in academia, they have been relegated to an interpretive community, which says and understands the world one way, but lives in it by recursively organizing and reproducing the agential moments of the American Protestant capitalist social structure.
3. Du Bois quoted in, Hunton, Alphaeus w. (1970). "W.E.B. Du Bois: the meaning of his life," Pp. 131–137. In *Black Titan: W.E.B. Du Bois*, Edited by John Henrik Clarke et al. Boston: Beacon Press.

Chapter Eight

Fait Accompli

The rise of Barack Obama to the Presidency of the United States of America is not a symbol of either the potentiality of the African subject in America, or the diversity of the society. Instead, it symbolizes the end-goal of the white man's burden and will, to self-consciously dominate and shape everything and everyone to his will and in his own image and likeness in fulfillment of establishing a Protestant patriarchal theocracy on earth to await the second coming of Jesus Christ. The identity or practical consciousness of the black American today is a paragon for the devastation, deculturalization, and inhumanity that accompanied this burden and quest of whites under the umbrella of their Protestantism as embodied and expressed through the ideological apparatuses of the modern American nation-state and concomitantly contemporary global institutions such as the IMF, World Bank, and the United Nations, which were established to globally do to (subjugate, oppress, deculturalize, and homogenize) the peoples' of color of the world what was done to the black American and American Indians.

The white Protestant bourgeois heterosexual male established their society and the "modern" world order, relationally, through the laws, religious doctrine, social categories, and other institutions embodied in the American nation-state system, thereby defining non-white, poor, homosexual, and females, "others," as infidels, heathens, heretics, or nonbelievers, who, within the social categories they were categorized, were terrorized, murdered, discriminated against, and marginalized. The response of the "others" to this terrorism and marginalization, guised under the purposive rationality of a "non-ideological," "disenchanted" "evolutionary" "modernizing" ethos (re) presented as the "rational" nature of reality and existence as such, was multiple and diverse, but as in the case of the majority of black Americans, for example, their acceptance of the social categories, and the "evolutionary" and "rational" structural terms of the white bourgeois Protestant power elite led to their desire to avoid "traditionalism," murder, discrimination, and marginalization, and achieve equality of opportunity, distribution, and recognition with their white counterparts by recursively organizing and reproducing the identity or practical consciousness of whites in a hybrid form, alas the liberal black Protestant heterosexual bourgeois male identity, that became a subversive-less simulacrum of white bourgeois heterosexual patriarchal Protestantism which stood against, and attempted to incorporate, "other" black responses to discrimination and marginalization, within their relational logic.

This hybrid, black, simulacrum of white bourgeois heterosexual patriarchal Protestant identity defined by its liberal aim for equality of opportunity and recognition amidst terrorism, murder, marginalization, and discrimination is neither a revolutionary and subversive identity, nor does it speak to the heterogeneity of cultural identity within modern American society. Instead, it highlights two things about the social psychological nature of individual being-in-the-world within the structure of modern society: first, as Louis Althusser so brilliantly pointed out in his famous essay, "Ideology and Ideological State Apparatuses," there is "no subject but by and for their subjection"; and second, and this is tied to the aforementioned Althusserian dictum that social psychological identity is associated with power and domination, societies, including modern American society, whether primitive or modern, up to this point in the human archaeological record, has never been heterogeneous or democratic because it is so constituted based on two opposing forces, marginalization and integration.

Be that as it may, identity, or, more broadly, consciousness formation, as argued here, is the sense of individuality or subjectness of the mind determined and negated, as Theodor Adorno points out, by society through, in Foucaultian terms, its "manifold forms of domination," i.e., power relations. This means in contemporary times, the "manifold forms of domination" by which the "modernizing ethos" of capital or the purposive-rationality of white bourgeois heterosexual Protestant men coming out of the West (America in particular) sought and seeks to universalize their identity and form of social relation all in the attempt to (re) produce surplus value (economic gain) on a global scale (Wallerstein, 1982). The Althusserian problematic of this sociocultural turn in identity or consciousness formation—that is, the view that race and ethnicity, culture, and identity are not determined by biology but are instead sociohistorical constructs based on institutionalized power relations—has been raised by post-colonial theorists. This problematic centers on the notion of the heterogeneity/hybridity of the subjected individual and whether or not those who have been oppressed (subaltern) or discriminated against on account of their "distinct" identity, i.e., "other" form of being-in-the-world, from the "practical consciousness" or hegemony of the determining global (American) Protestant capitalist social structural (i.e., societal) framework, have a distinct identity or consciousness from which to utter confrontational words against their white bourgeois Protestant oppressors. Homi Bhabha and Gayatri Chakravorty Spivak, whose writings represent the two divergent views, are also the two most outstanding postcolonial scholars on these subjects.

THE BHABHA AND SPIVAK DEBATE

Reasoning from a psychoanalytic and poststructural understanding of the colonizer/colonized relationship by which bourgeois capital once marginalized the world's people of color in order to constitute its own "pure" liberal bourgeois "modern" national identity and accumulate surplus-value, Bhabha and Spivak, respectively, reason that the *post*colonial subject or individual is inevitably heterogeneous. However, whereas for Bhabha this heterogeneity is created within a "liminal space" wherein postcolonial subjects (hybrids) can utter confrontational words by becoming a "speaking subject" with their "gaze back upon the eye of power" as opposed to a "silent native" with their gaze deferred, for Spivak, this is not the case and the "unrepresentable" heterogeneous "subaltern" cannot speak. In other words, for the psychoanalytically minded Bhabha (1995) this means, in terms of the colonizer/colonized social relationship by which the power elites, white bourgeois Protestant heterosexual men, of modernity constituted their liberal bourgeois national "modern" discourse against backward and traditional "others" of the world, which they murdered, marginalized, discriminated against, and exploited in order to usurp their resources and accumulate profits, that there is a "split between its [(imperialist law and education)] appearance as original and authoritative and its articulation as repetition and difference" . . . (Bhabha, 1995: 32). In this instance, he goes on to point out, "[w]hat is articulated in the doubleness of colonial discourse is not the violence of one powerful nation writing out another [but] a mode of contradictory utterance that ambivalently re-inscribes both colonizer and colonized" (Quoted in Parry, 1995: 42). This ambivalence, accordingly, defers authenticity, making cultural utterances indeterminant, dynamic, and heterogeneous, and provides the "liminal space" from which the "other" or *post*colonial subject (hybrid) can become a "speaking subject" through, and, at times, against the discourse of the colonizer given that power is revealed to be something that it is not, socially constructed as opposed to natural.

Spivak, "Can the Subaltern Speak" (1995), reasoning along a poststructural line, concludes, contrary to Bhabha, "imperialism's epistemic bellicosity decimated the old culture and left the colonized without the ground from which they could utter confrontational words . . ."(Parry, 1995: 43); thus, "[t]he subaltern cannot speak" (Spivak, 1994 [1988]: 104). That is, "[i]n subaltern studies, because of the violence of imperialist epistemic, social, and disciplinary inscription, a project understood in essentialist terms must traffic in a radical textual practice of differences" (Spivak, 1995 [1988]: 27), for "the colonized subaltern is irretrievably heterogeneous" (Spivak, 1995 [1988]: 26) given their relation to, and representation by, the colonizer. Therefore, "[f]or the 'true' subaltern group, whose identity is its [(represented)] difference, there is no unrepresentable subaltern subject that can know and speak itself . . ." (Spivak, 1994 [1988]: 80). In the case of the third world woman, which is her example in the work above, "[b]etween patriarchy and imperialism, subject-constitution and object-formation, the figure of the woman disappears, not into a pristine nothingness, but into a violent shuttling which is the displaced figuration of the 'third-world woman' caught between tradition and modernization" (Spivak, 1994 [1988]: 102).

THE PROBLEMATIC

The modernity or modernization Spivak and Bhabha highlights as the determinant of postcolonial identity emphasizes the integration, by white bourgeois Protestant men, of the world into a functional system "based on capitalist commodity production organized by a world market in which both purely economic competitive advantage and political interference by states play an interactive role" against the parochialism and traditionalism of primitive societies (Chase-Dunn, 1977: 455). In other words, "in the modern world-system there is only one mode of production, commodity production for profit on the world market, that articulates different forms of labor exploitation and encompasses a system of differentially powerful [(core)] states and peripheral areas" (Chase-Dunn, 1977: 455) from whom concessions are extracted and social relations are normalized, regardless of race, ethnicity, gender, and sexuality, to meet the ends (profit-motive) of the capitalist system as driven by one powerful core state, the colonizing hegemon. In today's global setting the national bourgeoisie of the US, in alliance with Europe, being that hegemon.

Whereas the dominant focus of world-systems analysis tends to be on the exploitative capitalist material relations among and within core and periphery states, i.e., *systems* integration; the point of emphasis for postcolonial thinkers like Spivak and Bhabha is on the ideological (racial and national) aspect or the *social* integration of this relation, in terms of capitalist ideological (racial and national) domination, by white bourgeois Protestant men. This is an important distinction in terms of understanding the origins and nature of identity and identity politics within bourgeois liberal Protestant national ideology whose power elite, white and hybrid liberal bourgeois heterosexual Protestants, sees the system or structure of capitalist social relations as "organically" distinct (a public sphere) from the plethora of traditional and postcolonial cultural meanings and subjective experiences, which operate within its rational and "organic" systemic framework (public sphere) within a private sphere of the lifeworld that is not colonized by the former.

Bhabha through his notion of hybridity supports this "liberal national" modern bourgeois viewpoint, which makes a distinction between the public and private spheres of human interaction in "modernity." The Bhabhaian hybrid operates within the systemic framework (public sphere) of global capitalism by becoming a speaking "modern other subject" (i.e., an "embourgeoised" hybrid) with their gaze back upon the eye of power against the traditionalism of those "others" of the private sphere by which they are (re) presented by power.

The postcolonial position assumed by Spivak, in somewhat keeping with the social structural determinism of the world-system school, implies that the contrary is the norm. That is, the capitalist system, and its structural logic and ethic, colonizes the lifeworld—the world of day-to-day practical action of the private sphere—through institutional and ideological apparatuses to prevent differentiation of norms and subjective experiences from the integrative agential moments associated with the purposive-rationality of the "Protestant ethic and the spirit of capitalism." Hence, the subaltern can not speak because the private sphere is itself colonized, and therefore leaves no space for alternative discourses, which, although they arise because of the indeterminacy of meaning in ego-centered communicative discourse, are discriminated against and marginalized to delimit and integrate the discourse of power as embodied in the purposive-rationality of the elites of the public sphere.

From this Spivakian structural determining "mechanical" position wherein the discourse of modernity is constituted through the marginalization of difference or the representable subject constitution of the traditional "other," the view, is that globalizing capitalist core states, like the US (i.e., the hegemon of the contemporary world-system), do not rely exclusively on political and military force, as in the heydays of colonialism, to extract concessions, or market forces for that matter to reproduce the system or the structure of capitalist social relations amongst their citizens and those in periphery nations. Instead, as governing elites in control of the state, as the constitutive element or apparatus for bourgeois domination and subject constitution, investors, white and hybrid liberal bourgeois Protestant heterosexual men, pressure other states to use state "ideological apparatuses" such as education and the political process to *interpellate* and *embourgeois* their "workers and other citizens" with the "modern" identity and ideological practices that justifies, and makes acceptable, their role in the investor/worker relationship that structures the global social relation of production (Althusser, 2001 [1971]) against the representable object formation and subject constitution of the traditional "other." In other words, through "ideological state apparatuses," such as education, politics, language, etc. social actors in modern societies are named (interpellated) and given ("embourgeoised" with) the modern "ethics" and "practical-consciousness" needed for both their "ontological security" and the reproduction of the structural identities and practices needed for the mode of production by which capital (investors of white and hybrid liberal bourgeois Protestant heterosexual men and women) seeks to generate surplus-value at the expense of the masses (workers) in possession of their labor power and "other" possible alternative "traditional" ways of "Being-in-the-world" or object formations and subject constitutions which are discriminated against and marginalized to integrate the dominant discourse.

Thus, "ideological state apparatuses," in essence, become the force-less means of enculturation or socialization to the dominant capitalist Protestant order of things, and prevent differentiation of thought and action. This fact further implies that the transformation of society rests not on the subjective initiatives of *all* social actors, but on the "modern" purposive rationality, disseminated through education, language, and politics as ideological apparatuses, which (US) capital (contemporarily) equates with the nature of reality and existence as such. Hence, whereas those in power positions, investors in the global economy, actively partake in the reproduction and transformation of society and the world around them, by (re) configuring the discursive practices (i.e., rules and regulations of the "Spirit of Capitalism") of the ideology within which their self-interest is best attainable, the majority of "others," interpellated as workers and other citizens (non-investors), at best, become pawns of the ideology, as they recursively organize and reproduce, for their ontological security, the discursive practices of power. This is a seemingly non-agential and oppressive position, for from this perspective social actors lack the theoretical and practical skills to transform their world as they encounter it, they simply reproduce it (attempting to live as investors) given their indoctrination—"embourgeoisement," in state ideological apparatuses such as education—into the pragmatics of bourgeois living, which exploits and oppresses the many for the expense of the few seeking economic gain for its own sake.

Spivak, from this determinist standpoint, is correct to see that the "shuttling between tradition and modernization" leaves most subalterns unspeakable from the "un-represented" represented grounds, i.e., "tradition," from which they "originally" encountered the capitalist colonizer. However, it is not the case, as she concludes, that the encounter with the latter and its heteronomously prescribed and represented heterogeneous subjectivity is *in fact* (in the material practical sense) heterogeneous, nor does it leave the subalterns, who have encountered its "epistemic bellicosity," unspeakable.[1] More concretely, for example, it is not the case because blacks are represented by bourgeois power as a structurally differentiated group known as lazy and impetuous "black workers," they have a pragmatic "identity-in-differential" to that of white power grounded in their "blackness," which they recursively organize and reproduce as their "practical consciousness" against dominant white bourgeois Protestant identity (thrifty, pious, etc.). To the contrary, once interpellated and socialized or "embourgeoised" in the ideological and disciplining order of the colonizer, all, as Homi Bhabha points out with his "hybridity" construct, are able to speak as "embourgeoised others" (hybrids) given the ambivalence (the desire to prove self worth along the lines of the society's purposive rationale against the contempt to which they are subject as a representable "other") by which the hybrid identity (i.e., the black bourgeoisie) is (re) produced. The problem from this standpoint is not the unspeakability and unrepresentability of the subject. But what they say, how they say it, why it is said, and the representation by power of the utterances: heterogeneous, which is a result of the deferment of meaning and ego-centered communicative discourse, and problematic, or "hybrid" and unproblematic.

In more empirical and contemporary terms, in other words, whether colonized or otherwise, all subjects, "speaking embourgeoised hybrid subjects," as in the case of Bhabha, Spivak, W.E.B. Du Bois, and President Barack Obama, or "silent natives" as in the case of Fidel Castro of Cuba and "fundamentalist Islam" with their gazed deferred from the eye of power, as it stands today, partake in a heteronomous order (the societal arrangements associated with the purposive-rationality of global capitalist development) that relationally, along the lines of Hegel's master/slave dialectic, produces and reproduces heterogeneous identities, which participate in the ideological totality of the capitalist societal order as "representable backward or traditional others," in order to delimit its "pure" dominant "modern" identity, i.e., rational calculating agents of the Protestant ethic and the spirit of capitalism. This dialectical relationship, as Spivak rightly points out, therefore, gives everyone, as a structurally differentiated representable "other," "classes-in-themselves," a voice into what they can and cannot say (and where they can say it) within the order. The problem with this position is that "true" heterogeneous identities, what Karl Marx referred to as "classes-for-themselves" as opposed to the in-themselves created by structural differentiation, are plausible only if every prescribed and represented identity turned their gaze inward away from the eye of power in order to establish a "self-representable" order or "practical consciousness" based on the prescribed and represented "other" identity against the attempt to assume the "pure" modern identity of power as a representable "other" or hybrid. In this instance, the idea of a subaltern being unable to speak would be a result of one heteronomous order or object formation oppressing and representing another in an attempt to efface their ideological and practical foundation, for example, America's contemporary or postcolonial efforts against Communist Cuba and the Islamic "fundamentalist" world.

America's acrimonious relationship with communist Cuba and contemporary Islamic fundamentalist movements in today's modern or "post-modern" capitalist world system represents the nature of this colonizer/colonized, master/slave, self/other, subject/object constituting relationship, in a *post*colonial" context, by which capital constitutes its "pure" liberal and national bourgeois identity, one heteronomous order attempting to rewrite and represent the ideological and practical foundations of a subject of another order; while the discourses of W.E.B. Du Bois, President Barack Obama, Homi Bhabha, and Spivak represent the nature of the speaking *post*colonial "modern" world, hybrids or elite "others," who embody the interests and "practical consciousness" of their former colonizers, continuing, through the ideological apparatuses of the nation-state, to rewrite the ideological and practical foundations of, and for, their once colonized masses through a secular or liberal and national discourse of the Protestant ethic and the spirit of capitalism, i.e., "secular modernity." The latter as (re) presented by the power agents of American global capitalism is unproblematic given their speakability as modernized hybrid "others," i.e., "classes-in-themselves," who are not seeking the institutionalization of a new ethos, or "object formation and subject constitution," but the participation of their "embourgeoised hybrid" modern identification in the recognizable order of things, i.e., "secular modernity." (I would venture to argue this is the driving attempt by the US in Iraq and Afghanistan, to establish a secular state controlled by hybrids or Islamic modernists over "other" object formations and subject constitutions). The formers, communist Cuba and fundamentalist Islam, on the contrary, given their attempts to institutionalize the practice of their ethos as "classes-for-themselves," are represented by the power elites of the American dominated capitalist world-system or empire as an "axis of evil" that threatens the object formation and subjective identity of modernity. Communist Cuba attempts to do so by convicting the secular liberal discourse of modernity coming out of the West of not identifying with itself and therefore seeks to institutionalize a more perfect secular modernity or a totalitarian "traditional" type grounded in the "dialectic of enlightenment" as suggested and represented by American power. On the contrary, Islamic fundamentalists (i.e., Egyptian Muslim Brothers, Al Qeida, Islamic Salvation Front, Iran, Osama Bin Laden, the Taliban, etc.), who for the most part categorically reject the Western liberal national model, see the socializing ethos (i.e., "the Protestant ethic and the spirit of capitalism") of modernity as an illegitimate non-identity, which opposes their "traditional" Islamic cosmological identity. The same historic identity, which was allowed to maintain its legitimation under the support of American hegemony during the Cold War, which they (America) now represent as a "traditional" backward world-view that threatens contemporary "modern" Western Civilization (Moaddel, 2005: 1–25).[2]

DISCUSSION

In terms of the social integration of society and human identity, contemporarily, these are the two phenomena taking place in the world under the hegemony of the American dominated capitalist state-driven World-system. On the one hand, you have a set of Islamic societies and identities (Iran, Syria, Algeria, Egypt, the Taliban, Al Qeida) that are, in order to integrate and constitute their societies, contemporarily, turning their gaze inward but are reproducing the master/slave, subject/object, or Self/Other dialectic by following the lead of their former capitalist colonizers in stratifying or structurally differentiating society economically, racially, and gender-wise based fundamentally on Islamic cosmological doctrine (Moaddel, 2005: 5). On the other hand, you have poor "developing" formerly colonized nations in the Caribbean, for example, who attempt to turn their gaze inward like communist Cuba in order to resolve the internal contradictions of capital accumulation, but given the fact that their nation-state is ideologically controlled by "embourgeoised hybrid" others, who recursively attempt to organize and reproduce the protestant structure of signification through the spirit of capitalism (neoliberal policy), they turn their gaze back upon the eye of power (United States and Europe) for recognition. What we have in those societies (Jamaica, St. Lucia, Barbados, Grenada, etc.) is an exact replica of the social relations of production of the contemporary capitalist social structure in which a bourgeois "national" minority (hybrids) controls the state and its ideological apparatuses in order to sell (interpellate them in the order of things as individual laborers) the majority of the people to the highest global capitalist bidder.

In the two cases, the former, as driven by Islamist fundamentalists over the objections of their "embourgeoised hybrid" liberal and nationalist counterparts (Arab nationalists, communists, and Islamic modernists, i.e., Jordan) seeking to institutionalize a "secular" Islamic modernity in a national position of their own, offers the most promising potential for social change and liberation of the oppressed created by the crisis (proletarianization, ecological devastation, etc.,) in capitalist accumulation, for they prescribe an underlying ontology that, in a Weberian sense, if given the potential to purposively rationalize its Islamic cosmological ethos along the lines of the protestant ethic, can challenge the exploitation and oppression of man by man that a variant of the Protestant ethic gives rise to in its structural, secular practice, the spirit of capitalism. These contemporary Islamicists, represented in the figure of Osama Bin Laden and the clergy-centered discourse of the Iranian state, for examples, just like Marxists, understand the intrusive materiality of Western capitalism as a cultural medium, a meaningful thing, not use betrayed by exchange but the sacred profaned (Friedland, 2002: 401). However, the mere fact that these emerging Islamic power elites seek to masculinize the public sphere, to contain the erotic energies of heterosexuality within the family; this, according to western and "postcolonial" hybrid elites, has resulted in the subjugation of women a critical source for political mobilization and societal development: thus reconstituting society along the master/slave dialectic wherein women, homosexuals, liberal Islamicists, Arab nationalists and communists, and Westerners become the objects of subjugation and oppression. If these power elites take into consideration the internal contradictions of their attempt, as is taking place in Iran, while holding on to their anathema for the spirit of capitalism inherent in their Islamic fundamentalist ideology and practices, there is potential in their efforts to turn their gaze inward and reconstitute the contemporary American dominated world-system constituted by bourgeois "Protestant" ideology.[3] However, so long as their movement against the racial, class, and consumerist basis of the American dominated contemporary world-system is itself grounded in the oppression of American supporters, hybrid elites, women, homosexuals, etc., radical Islamists will never move beyond the primitive "mechanical solidarity" by which they constitute their practical consciousnesses, for they will continue to be discriminated against and marginalized as a backward traditional "other" worldview by the western and "postcolonial" hybrid elites of modernity in order to constitute their own "liberal modern bourgeois Protestant practical consciousness."

In the latter case, the case of the black American, represented in the person of Barack Hussein Obama, is illustrative of the subversive-less nature of the *post*colonial hybrid and the inability of modernity (i.e., the black American as the embodiment of the articulator principles of modernity), contrary to Jürgen Habermas's (1984, 1987) "organic" liberal position, to resolve its own contradictions.

Black Americans subjectified/objectified in the "Protestant Ethic and the spirit of capitalism" of American society was completely subjectified and subjugated on account of race and class position (Mocombe, 2004). W.E.B Du Bois relying on the racial and national ideology of the late nineteenth and early twentieth century conceived of the ambivalence that arose in him, as a result of the "class racism" (Étienne Balibar's term) of American society, as a double consciousness: "two souls," "two thoughts," in the Negro whose aim is to merge these two thoughts into one distinct way of being, i.e., to be whole again.

> After the Egyptian and Indian, the Greek and Roman, the Teuton and Mongolian, the Negro is a sort of seventh son, born with a veil, and gifted with second-sight in this American world, —a world which yields him no true self-consciousness, but only lets him see himself through the revelation of the other world. It is a peculiar sensation, this double-consciousness, this sense of always looking at one's self through the eyes of others, of measuring one's soul by the tape of a world that looks on in amused contempt and pity. One ever feels his twoness,—an American, a Negro; two souls, two thoughts, two unreconciled strivings; two warring ideals in one dark body, whose dogged strength alone keeps it from being torn asunder.
>
> The history of the American Negro is the history of this strife, —this longing to attain self conscious manhood, to merge his double self into a better and truer self. In this merging he wishes neither of the older selves to be lost. He would not Africanize America, for America has too much to teach the world and Africa. He would not bleach his Negro soul in a flood of white Americanism, for he knows that Negro blood has a message for the world. He simply wishes to make it possible for a man to be both a Negro and an American, without being cursed and spit upon by his fellows, without having the doors of Opportunity closed roughly in his face.
>
> This, then, is the end of his striving: to be a coworker in the kingdom of culture, to escape both death and isolation, to husband and use his best powers and his latent genius (Du Bois, 1995 [1903]: 45–47).

This double-consciousness Du Bois alludes to, in this famous passage of his work *The Souls of Black Folk*, is not a metaphor for the racial duality of black American life in America. Instead, it speaks to Du Bois's, as a black liberal bourgeois Protestant man, ambivalence about the society because it prevents him from exercising his true American consciousness because of the society's anti-liberal and discriminatory practices, which overtime forced Du Bois to adopt "pan-African communism" against his early beliefs in liberal bourgeois Protestantism, which Obama contemporarily subscribes to.

Contrary to Du Bois's later "pan-African communist" message against assimilation, to make themselves whole the majority of black Americans, like Obama, did not establish (by averting their gaze from the eye of power) a new object formation or totality, based on the "message" of their people, which spoke against racial and class stratification and would have produced heterogeneity into the American capitalist bourgeois world-system; instead, since there was no other "message" but that of the society which turned and represented the "original" African message of their people into inarticulate, animalistic backward gibberish, they (blacks) turned their gaze back upon the eye of power (through protest and success in their endeavors) for recognition as "speaking subjects" of the society. Power hesitantly responded by allowing some of them (the hybrid modern "other") to partake in the order of things, which gave rise to the black identity, the liberal black bourgeoisie or hybrids, of Obama, which delimits the desired agential moments of the social structure for all blacks (Frazier, 1957; Hare, 1965 [1991]; Woodson, 1933 [1969]; Kardiner, 1962 [1951).

Thus black protest as a structurally differentiated "class-in-itself" (black underclass) within the American protestant bourgeois order, unlike Communist Cuba's protest which sought to institutionalized a more perfect modernity based on their structurally differentiated proletarian identity, did not reconstitute American society, but integrated the black subjects, whose ideals and practices (acquired in ideological apparatuses, i.e., schools, law, churches (black and white)), as speaking subjects, were that of the larger society, i.e., the protestant ethic, into its exploitative and oppressive order—an order which promotes a debilitating performance principle actualized through calculating rationality, which may result in economic gain for its own sake for a few predestined individuals.

CONCLUSION

Essentially, just as in the case of communist Cuba, the Frankfurt school's "Negative Dialectics" represents the means by which the Du Bois of *The Souls*, President Barack Obama, and the majority of liberal bourgeois black Americans, who led the integrationist movement, confronted their historical situation. The difference between the means by which contemporary Islamist are going about their fight against the "modernizing ethos" of global "national" capitalism, and the negative dialectics of Communist Cuba, the Du Bois of *The Souls*, President Obama, and the black American liberal bourgeoisie or hybrid is subtle, but the consequences are enormously obvious.

For the Frankfurt school, "[t]o proceed dialectically means to think in contradictions, for the sake of the contradiction once experienced in the thing, and against that contradiction. A contradiction in reality, it is a contradiction against reality" (Adorno, 1973 [1966]: 145). This is the ongoing dialectic they call "Negative Dialectics:"

> Totality is to be opposed by convicting it of nonidentity with itself—of the nonidentity it denies, according to its own concept. Negative dialectics is thus tied to the supreme categories of identitarian philosophy as its point of departure. Thus, too, it remains false according to identitarian logic: it remains the thing against which it is conceived. It must correct itself in its critical course—a course affecting concepts which in negative dialectics are formally treated as if they came "first" for it, too (Adorno, 1973 [1966]: 147).

This position, as Adorno points out, is problematic in that the identitarian class convicting the totality of which it is apart remains the thing against which it is conceived. Hence communist Cuba is not an "identity-in-differential" to modernity, but a paragon of the modernizing project. As in the case of black Americans, their "negative dialectics," their awareness of the contradictions of the heteronomous racial capitalist order did not foster a reconstitution of that order but a request that the order rid itself of a particular contradiction and allow their participation in the order, devoid of that particular contradiction, which prevented them from identifying with the totality, i.e., that all men are created equal except the enslaved black American. The end result of this particular protest was in the reconfiguration of society (or the totality) in which those who exercised its reified consciousness, irrespective of skin-color, could partake in its order.

In essence, the contradiction, as interpreted by blacks, was not in the "pure" identity of the heteronomous order, which is reified as reality and existence as such, but in the praxis (as though praxis and structure are distinct) of the individuals, i.e., institutional regulators or power elites, who only allowed the participation of blacks within the order of things because they were "speaking subjects" (i.e., hybrids, who recursively organized and reproduced the agential moments of the social structure) as opposed to "silent natives" (i.e., Nation of Islam, who were and are still "others"). And herein rests the problem with attempting to reestablish an order simply based on what appears to be the contradictory practices of a reified consciousness. For in essence the totality is not "opposed by convicting it of nonidentity with itself—of the nonidentity it denies, according to its own concept," but on the contrary, the particular is opposed by the constitutive subjects for not exercising its total identity. In the case of liberal black bourgeois America, the totality, American racial capitalist society, was opposed through a particularity, i.e., racism, which stood against their bourgeois identification with the whole. In such a case, the whole remains superior to its particularity, and it functions as such.

In order to go beyond this "mechanical" dichotomy, i.e., whole/part, subject/object, master/slave, universal/particular, society/individual, etc., by which society or more specifically the object formation of modernity up till this point in the human archaeological record has been constituted, so that society can be reconstituted wherein "Being" (Dasein) is nonsubjective and nonobjective, "organic" in the Habermasian sense, it is necessary, as Adorno points out, that the totality (which is not a "thing in itself") be opposed, not however, as he sees it, "by convicting it of nonidentity with itself" as in the case of black America and communist Cuba, but by identifying it as a non-identity identity that does not have the "natural right" to dictate identity in an absurd world with no inherent meaning or purpose except those which are constructed by social actors operating within a sacred metaphysic. This is not what happened in black America or in many "modernizing" nation-states under the leadership of *post*colonial hybrids such as the Du Bois of *The Souls* and Barack Obama, but one can suggests, against conventional readings which view Islamic fundamentalism either as a reaction to modern secular discourse or the product of the "totalitarian despots" of nation-states in the middle east (Moaddel, 2005: 343), that this is what is taking place in the Islamic fundamentalist world (i.e., Iran) today within the hegemony of the American dominated capitalist world-system.

The liberal black American by identifying with the totality, which Adorno rightly argues is a result of the "universal rule of forms," the idea that "a consciousness that feels impotent, that has lost confidence in its ability to change the institutions and their mental images, will reverse the conflict into identification with the aggressor" (Adorno, 1973 [1966]: 94), reconciled their double consciousness, i.e., the ambivalence that arises as a result of the conflict between subjectivity and forms (objectivity), by becoming "hybrid" Americans desiring to exercise the "pure" identity of the American totality and reject the contempt to which they were and are subject. The contradiction of slavery in the face of equality—the totality not identifying with itself—was seen as a manifestation of individual practices, since subjectively they were part of the totality, and not an absurd way of life inherent in the logic of the totality. Hence, their protest was against the practices of the totality, not the totality itself, since that would mean denouncing the consciousness that made them whole. Just the same, the "embourgeoised hybrid" leaderships of nation-states today do not question the totality of modernity, they simply, if they do at all, question its particular failures, i.e., mainly, given the declining significance of race, class oppression. On the contrary, contemporary Islamic fundamentalist identitarian movements (i.e., Iran, Taliban, Al Qeida, Algeria), which during the Cold War were legitimized by the power elites of the American social structure to defeat communists and left wing forces in the Middle East (Moaddel , 2005; Tabb, 2005), have decentered or "convicted" the totality of American modernity, which today represents them as an "other," not for not identifying with itself, but as an adverse "sacred-profaned" cultural possibility against their own "God-ordained" possibility (alternative object formation), which they are attempting to exercise in the world. However, that the Islamists have reconceptualized the signifiers of their subjugators along a patriarchal and heterosexual sacred communalism, they, according to American and hybrid power, have reinstituted another "mechanical" form of domination, along the master/slave and self/other, which seeks to subjugate and avow inequalities of opportunities as opposed to an "organic" solidarity constituted through mutually agreed upon rules of conduct which are sanctioned amongst various diverse groups as supposedly "represented" in liberal bourgeois institutions.

NOTES

1. Spivak, by assuming the subaltern's difference, contrary to her rhetoric, assigns them a supposedly unrepresentable "identity-in-differential" to that of the hybrid elites who speak the colonizer. How is that possible? Unless there are fully visible alternative speaking subjects who happened to be a distinct "community of subalterns."

2. Mansoor Moaddel (2005), *Islamic Modernism, Nationalism, and Fundamentalism: Episode and Discourse*, posits that Islamic Fundamentalism in, for example, "Algeria, Egypt, Iran, and Syria originated from the monolithic discursive context imposed from above by an intrusive secular ideological state. The state's extensive interventions in culture politicized culture production and resulted in the formulation of political Islam" (Moaddel, 2005: 292). My position argues that Islamic fundamentalism is the result of the on-going strife between an historical interpretive Islamic fundamentalist community directed by Islamic cosmological doctrine fighting against the presence of Western power backing and operating through the "modernist" rulers of Islamic states (i.e., Jordan and present-day Iraq). This position views the internal power struggles amongst followers of Islam as a historical parallel to the Protestant power struggles (Calvinists vs. Puritans, etc.) of the late 15th and early 16th century.

3. This implies, thinking negatively ("negative dialectics) within their own Islamic cosmology as opposed to that of the Protestant ethic and the spirit of capitalism which "enframes" modernity.

References Cited

Adorno, Theodor W. (2000). *Negative Dialectics*. New York: Continuum.
Allen, Ernest Jr. (2002). "Du Boisian Double Consciousness: The Unsustainable Argument." *The Massachusetts Review*, 43 (2): 217–253.
Allen, Ernest Jr. (1992). "Ever Feeling One's Twoness: 'Double Ideals and 'Double Consciousness' in the Souls of Black Folk." *Critique of Anthropology*, 12 (3): 261–275.
Allen, Richard L. (2001). *The Concept of Self: A Study of Black Identity and Self Esteem*. Detroit: Wayne State University Press.
Althusser, Louis (2001). *Lenin and Philosophy and Other Essays*. New York: Monthly Review Press.
Althusser, Louis and Étienne Balibar (1970). *Reading Capital* (Ben Brewster, Trans.). London: NLB.
Altschuler, Richard (ed.) (1998). *The living Legacy of Marx, Durkheim, and Weber: Applications and Analyses of Classical Sociological Theory by Modern Social Scientists*. New York: Gordian Knot Books.
Appiah, Anthony (1985). "The Uncompleted Argument: Du Bois and the Illusion of Race." *Critical Inquiry*, 12: 21–37.
Aptheker, Herbert (ed.) (1985). *W.E.B. Du Bois Against Racism: Unpublished Essays, Papers, Addresses, 1887–1961*. Amherst: The University of Massachusetts Press.
Archer, Margaret S. (1985). "Structuration versus Morphogenesis." In H.J. Helle and S.N. Eisenstadt (Eds.), *Macro-Sociological Theory: Perspectives on Sociological Theory* (Volume 1) (pp. 58–88). United Kingdom: J.W. Arrowsmith Ltd.
Asante, Molefi Kete (1988). *Afrocentricity*. New Jersey: Africa World.
Asante, Molefi K. (1990a). *Kemet, Afrocentricity and Knowledge*. New Jersey: Africa World.
Asante, Molefi K. (1990b). "African Elements in African-American English." In Joseph E. Holloway (Ed.), *Africanisms in American Culture* (pp. 19–33). Bloomington and Indianapolis: Indiana University Press.

Austin, J.L. (1997). *How to do Things With Words* (Second edition, J.O. Urmson and Marina Sbisà, editors). Cambridge, Massachusetts: Harvard University Press.

Baker, Houston A., Jr. (1985). "The Black Man of Culture: W.E.B. Du Bois and The Souls of Black Folk." In William L. Andrews (Ed.), *Critical Essays on W.E.B. Du Bois* (pp.129–139). Boston: G.K. Hall & Co.

Balibar, Etienne & Immanuel Wallerstein (1991 [1988]). *Race, Nation, Class: Ambiguous Identities*. London: Verso.

Ballantine, Jeanne, H. (1993). *The Sociology of Education: A systematic Analysis* (3rd Edition). New Jersey: Prentice Hall.

Ball, Howard (2000). *The Bakke Case: Race, Education, and Affirmative Action*. Kansas: University Press of Kansas.

Barthes, Roland (1972). *Mythologies* (Annette Lavers, Trans.). New York: Hill and Wang.

Bell, Daniel (1985). *The Social Sciences Since the Second World War*. New Brunswick (USA): Transaction Books.

Bell, Bernard W. et al (editors) (1996). *W. E. B. Du Bois on Race and Culture: Philosophy, Politics, and Poetics*. New York and London: Routledge.

Bell, Bernard W. (1996). "Genealogical Shifts in Du Bois's Discourse on Double Consciousness as the Sign of African American Difference." In Bernard W. Bell et al (Eds.), *W.E.B. Du Bois on Race and Culture: Philosophy, Politics, and Poetics* (pp. 87–108). New York and London: Routledge.

Bell, Bernard W. (1985). "W.E.B. Du Bois's Struggle to Reconcile Folk and High Art." In William L. Andrews (Ed.), *Critical Essays on W.E.B. Du Bois* (pp.106–122). Andrews. Boston: G.K. Hall & Co.

Bennett, Lerone (1982). *Before the Mayflower*. Chicago: Johnson Publishing Company.

Bhabha, Homi (1995a). "Cultural Diversity and Cultural Differences." In Bill Ashcroft et al (Eds.), *The Post-colonial Studies Reader* (pp. 206–209). London and New York: Routledge.

Bhabha, Homi (1995b). "Signs Taken for Wonders." In Bill Ashcroft et al (Eds.), *The Post-colonial Studies Reader* (pp. 29–35). London and New York: Routledge.

Bhabha, Homi (1994). "Remembering Fanon: Self, Psyche and the Colonial Condition." In Patrick Williams and Laura Chrisman (Eds.), *Colonial Discourse and Post-Colonial Theory A Reader* (pp. 112–123). New York: Columbia University Press.

Billingsley, Andrew (1968). *Black Families in White America*. New Jersey: Prentice Hall.

Billingsley, Andrew (1970). "Black Families and White Social Science." *Journal of Social Issues*, 26, 127–142.

Billingsley, Andrew (1993). *Climbing Jacob's Ladder: The Enduring Legacy of African American Families*. New York: Simon & Schuster.

Bizzell, Patricia and Bruce Herzberg (2001). *The Rhetorical Tradition: Readings from Classical Times to the Present*. Boston: Bedford/St. Martin's.

Blassingame, John W. (1972). *The Slave Community: Plantation Life in the Antebellum South*. New York: Oxford University Press.

Boskin, Joseph (1965). "Race Relations in Seventeenth-Century America: The Problem of the Origins of Negro Slavery." In Donald Noel (Ed.), *The Origins of American Slavery and Racism* (pp. 95–105). Ohio: Charles E. Merrill Publishing Co.

Boswell, Terry (1989). "Colonial Empires and the Capitalist World-Economy: A Time Series Analysis of Colonization, 1640–1960." *American Sociological Review*, 54, 180–196.
Bourdieu, Pierre (1990). *The Logic of Practice* (Richard Nice, Trans.). Stanford, California: Stanford University Press.
Bourdieu, Pierre (1984). *Distinction: A Social Critique of the Judgement of Taste* (Richard Nice, Trans.). Cambridge MA: Harvard University Press.
Boxill, Bernard R. (1996). "Du Bois on Cultural Pluralism." In Bell W. Bernard et al (Eds.), *W.E.B. Du Bois on Race and Culture: Philosophy, Politics, and Poetics* (pp. 57–86). New York and London: Routledge.
Brecher, Jeremy and Tim Costello (1998). *Global Village or Global Pillage: Economic Reconstruction from the bottom up* (second ed.). Cambridge, Mass.: South End Press.
Brennan, Teresa (1997). "The Two Forms of Consciousness." *Theory Culture & Society*, 14 (4): 89–96.
Broderick, Francis L. (1959). *W.E.B. Du Bois, Negro Leader in a Time of Crisis*. Stanford, California: Stanford University Press.
Bruce, Dickinson D., Jr. (1992). "W.E.B. Du Bois and the Idea of Double Consciousness." *American Literature*, 64: 299–309.
Caws, Peter (1997). *Structuralism: A Philosophy for the Human Sciences*. New York: Humanity Books.
Chase-Dunn, Christopher and Peter Grimes (1995). "World-Systems Analysis." *Annual Review of Sociology*, 21, 387–417.
Chase-Dunn, Christopher and Richard Rubinson (1977). "Toward a Structural Perspective on the World-System." *Politics & Society*, 7: 4, 453–476.
Chase-Dunn, Christopher (1975). "The effects of international economic dependence on development and inequality: A cross-national study." *American Sociological Review*, 40, 720–738.
Clark, Robert P. (1997). *The Global Imperative: An Interpretive History of the Spread of Humankind*. Boulder, Colorado: Westview Press.
Clarke, John Henrik, et. al. (eds.) (1970). *Black Titan: W.E.B. Du Bois*. Boston: Beacon Press.
Cohen, J. (2002). *Protestantism and Capitalism: The Mechanisms of Influence*. New York: Aldine de Gruyter.
Collinson, Diane (1987). *Fifty Major Philosophers: A Reference Guide*. London: Routledge.
Coser, Lewis (1956). *The functions of social conflict*. New York: The Free Press.
Covino, William A. and David A. Jolliffe (1995). *Rhetoric: concepts, definitions, boundaries*. Needham Heights, Massachusetts: Allyn and Bacon.
Crothers, Charles (2003). "Technical Advances in General Sociological Theory: The Potential Contribution of Post-Structurationist Sociology." *Perspectives*, 26: 3, 3–6.
Crouch, Stanley (1993). "Who are We? Where Did We Come From? Where Are We Going?" In Gerald Early (Ed.), *Lure and Loathing: Essays on Race, Identity, and the Ambivalence of Assimilation* (pp. 80–94). New York: The Penguin Press.
Culler, Jonathan (1976). *Saussure*. Great Britain: Fontana/Collins.
Curtin, Philip D. (1969). *The Atlantic Slave Trade: A Census*. Madison, Wisconsin: The University of Wisconsin Press.

Dahrendorf, Ralf (1959). *Class and Class Conflict in Industrial Society.* Stanford, California: Stanford University Press.
Degler, Carl N. (1972). "Slavery and the Genesis of American Race Prejudice." In Donald Noel (Ed.), *The Origins of American Slavery and Racism* (pp. 59–80). Ohio: Charles E. Merrill Publishing Co.
DeMarco, Joseph P. (1983). *The Social Thought of W.E.B. Du Bois.* Lanham, MD: University Press of America.
Diop, Cheikh A. (1981). *Civilization or Barbarism: An Authentic Anthropology.* New York: Lawrence Hill Books.
Douglas, M. (1986). *How Institutions Think.* New York: Syracuse University Press.
Drake, St. Claire (1965). "The Social and Economic Status of the Negro in the United States." In Talcott Parsons and Kenneth B. Clark (Eds.), *The Negro American* (pp. 3–46). Boston: Houghton Mifflin Company.
Du Bois, W.E.B. (1995 [1903]). *The Souls of Black Folk.* New York: Penguin Putnam Inc.
Du Bois, W.E.B. (1984 [1940]). *Dusk of Dawn: An Essay toward an Autobiography of a Race Concept.* New Brunswick and London: Transaction Books.
Du Bois, W.E.B. (1971a [1897]). "The Conservation of Races." In Julius Lester (Ed.), *The Seventh Son: The Thought and Writings of W.E.B. Du Bois (Volume I)* (pp. 176–187). New York: Random House.
Du Bois, W.E.B. (1971b [1935]). "A Negro Nation Within The Nation." In Julius Lester (Ed.), *The Seventh Son: The Thought and Writings of W.E.B. Du Bois (Volume II)* (pp. 399–407). New York: Random House.
Du Bois, W.E.B. (1970 [1939]). *Black Folk, Then and Now: An Essay in the History and Sociology of the Negro Race.* New York: Octagon Books.
Du Bois, W. E. B. (1968). *The Autobiography of W.E.B. Du Bois: A Soliloquy on Viewing My Life from the Last Decade of its First Century.* US: International Publishers Co., Inc.
Du Bois, W.E.B. (1967 [1899]). *The Philadelphia Negro: A Social Study.* New York: Schocken Books.
Durkheim, Emile (1984 [1893]). *The Division of Labor in Society* (W.D. Halls, Trans.). New York: The Free Press.
Eagleton, Terry (1999). *Marx.* New York: Routledge.
Eagleton, Terry (1991). *Ideology: An Introduction.* London: Verso.
Early, Gerald (ed.) (1993). *Lure and Loathing: Essays on Race, Identity , and the Ambivalence of Assimilation.* New York: The Penguin Press.
Edgar, Andrew and Peter Sedgwick (Eds.) (1999). *Key Concepts in Cultural Theory.* London: Routledge.
Elkins, Stanley (1959). *Slavery: A Problem in American Institutional and Intellectual Life.* Chicago: University of Chicago Press.
Elkins, Stanley M. (1972). "The Dynamics of Unopposed Capitalism." In Donald Noel (Ed.), *The Origins of American Slavery and Racism* (pp. 45–58). Ohio: Charles E. Merrill Publishing Co.
Engels, Frederick (2000 [1884]. *The Origin of the Family, Private Property, and the State.* New York: Pathfinder Press.

Fanon, Frantz (1967). *Black Skin, White Masks* (Charles Lam Markmann, Trans.). New York: Grove Press.
Fanon, Frantz (1963). *The Wretched of the Earth* (Constance Farrington, Trans). New York: Grove Press.
Fogel, Robert W. (2003). *The Slavery Debates, 1952–1990: A Retrospective.* Baton Rouge: Louisiana State University Press.
Foner, Eric (1988). *Reconstruction: America's Unfinished Revolution 1863–1877.* New York: Harper&Row Publishers.
Foner, Eric (1990). *A Short History of Reconstruction 1863–1877.* New York: Harper&Row Publishers.
Foucault, Michel (1977). *Discipline and Punish: The Birth of the Prison* (Alan Sheridan, Trans.). London: Penguin Books.
Franklin, John Hope and Alfred A. Moss Jr. (2000). *From Slavery to Freedom: A History of African Americans* (Eighth Edition). New York: Alfred A. Knopf.
Fraser, Nancy (1997). Justice *Interruptus: Critical Reflections on the "Postsocialist" Condition.* New York & London: Routledge.
Frazier, Franklin E. (1939). *The Negro Family in America.* Chicago: University of Chicago Press.
Frazier, Franklin E. (1957). *Black Bourgeoisie: The Rise of a New Middle Class.* NewYork: The Free Press.
Frazier, Franklin E. (1968). *The Free Negro Family.* New York: Arno Press and The New York Times.
Freud, Sigmund (1989 [1940]). *An Outline of Psycho-Analysis* (James Strachey, Trans. and Editor). New York: W.W. Norton & Company.
Freud, Sigmund (1989 [1921]). *Group Psychology and the Analysis of the Ego* (James Strachey, Trans. and Editor). New York: W.W. Norton & Company.
Freud, Sigmund (1989 [1917]). *Introductory Lectures on Psycho-Analysis* (James Strachey, Trans. and Editor). New York: W.W. Norton & Company.
Gadamer, Hans-Georg (2002). *Truth and Method* (Second, Revised Edition, Joel Weinsheimer and Donald G. Marshall, Trans.). New York: Continuum.
Gartman, David (2002). "Bourdieu's Theory of Cultural Change: Explication, Application, Critique." *Sociological Theory* 20 (2): 255–277.
Gates, Henry L. et al. (Eds.) (1997). *The Norton Anthology: African America Literature.* New York: W.W. Norton & Company inc.
Gates, Henry Louis, Jr. and Cornel West (1996). *The Future of the Race.* New York: Vintage Books.
Geertz, Clifford (1973). *The Interpretation of Cultures.* New York: Basic Books.
Geertz, Clifford (2000). *Local Knowledge: Further Essays in Interpretive Anthropology.* New York: Basic Books.
Genovese, Eugene (1974). *Roll, Jordan, Roll.* New York: Pantheon Books.
Geronimus, Arline T. and F. Phillip Thompson. "To Denigrate, Ignore, or Disrupt: Racial Inequality in Health and the Impact of a Policy-induced Breakdown of African American Communities." *Du Bois Review* 1; 2: 247–279.
Giddens, Anthony (1984). *The Constitution of Society: Outline of the Theory of Structuration.* Cambridge: Polity Press.

Gilroy, Paul (1993). *The Black Atlantic: Modernity and Double Consciousness*. Cambridge, Massachusetts: Harvard.
Glazer, Nathan and Daniel P. Moynihan (1963). *Beyond the Melting Pot*. Cambridge: Harvard University Press.
Gooding-Williams, Robert (1996). "Outlaw, Appiah, and Du Bois's 'The Conservation of Races.'" In Bell W. Bernard et al. (Eds.), *W.E.B. Du Bois on Race and Culture: Philosophy, Politics, and Poetics* (pp. 39–56). New York and London: Routledge.
Gramsci, Antonio (1959). *The Modern Prince, and Other Writings*. New York: International Publishers.
Grutter v. Bollinger et al, 539 U.S. 02–241 (2003); 13 (Slip Opinion).
Gutiérrez, Ramón A. (2004). "Internal Colonialism: An American Theory of Race." *Du Bois Review*, 1; 2: 281–295.
Gutman, Herbert (1976). *The Black Family in Slavery and Freedom 1750–1925*. New York: Pantheon Books.
Habermas, Jürgen (1987). *The Theory of Communicative Action: Lifeworld and System: A Critique of Functionalist Reason* (Volume 2, Thomas McCarthy, Trans.). Boston: Beacon Press.
Habermas, Jürgen (1984). *The Theory of Communicative Action: Reason and the Rationalization of Society* (Volume 1, Thomas McCarthy, Trans.). Boston: Beacon Press.
Handlin, Oscar and Mary F. Handlin (1972). "The Origins of Negro Slavery." In Donald Noel (Ed.), *The Origins of American Slavery and Racism* (pp. 21–44). Ohio: Charles E. Merrill Publishing Co.
Harding, Vincent (1981). *There is a River: The Black Struggle for Freedom in America*. New York: Harcourt Brace & Company.
Hare, Nathan (1991). *The Black Anglo-Saxons*. Chicago: Third World Press.
Harris, Marvin. (1999). *Theories of culture in postmodern times*. Walnut Creek, California: AltaMira Press.
Harris, David R. and Jeremiah Joseph Sim (2002). "Who is Multiracial? Assessing the Complexity of Lived Race." *American Sociological Review* 67; 4: 614–627.
Hegel, G.W.F. (1977 [1807]). *Phenomenology of Spirit* (A.V. Miller, Trans.). Oxford: Oxford University Press.
Heidegger, Martin (1962 [1927]). *Being and Time*. New York: HarperSanFrancisco.
Helle, H.J. and S.N. Eisenstadt (ed.) (1985). *Macro-Sociological Theory: Perspectives on Sociological Theory* (Volume 1). United Kingdom: J.W. Arrowsmith Ltd.
Helle, H.J. and S.N. Eisenstadt (ed.) (1985). *Micro-Sociological Theory: Perspectives on Sociological Theory* (Volume 2). United Kingdom: J.W. Arrowsmith Ltd.
Herskovits, Melville J. (1958 [1941]). *The Myth of the Negro Past*. Boston: Beacon Press.
Hochschild, Jennifer L. (1984). *The New American Dilemma: Liberal Democracy and School Desegregation*. New Haven: Yale University Press.
Hogue, Lawrence W. (1996). *Race, Modernity, Postmodernity: A look at the History and the Literatures of People of Color Since the 1960s*. Albany: State University of New York Press.

Holloway, Joseph E. (ed.) (1990a). *Africanisms in American Culture*. Bloomington and Indianapolis: Indiana University Press.

Holloway, Joseph E. (1990b). "The Origins of African-American Culture." In Joseph Holloway (Ed.), *Africanisms in American Culture* (19–33). Bloomington and Indianapolis: Indiana University Press.

Holt, Thomas (1990). "The Political Uses of Alienation: W.E.B. Du Bois on Politics, Race, and Culture, 1903–1940." *American Quarterly* 42 (2): 301–323.

Horkheimer, Max and Theodor W. Adorno (2000 [1944]. *Dialectic of Enlightenment* (John Cumming, Trans.). New York: Continuum.

Horne, Gerald (1986). *Black and Red: W.E.B. Du Bois and the Afro-American Response to the Cold War, 1944–1963*. New York: State University of New York Press.

House, James S. (1977). "The Three Faces of Social Psychology." *Sociometry* 40: 161–177.

House, James S. (1981). "Social Structure and Personality." In Morris Rosenberg and Ralph Turner (Eds.), *Sociological Perspectives on Social Psychology* (pp. 525 561). New York: Basic Books.

Hudson, Kenneth and Andrea Coukos (2005). "The Dark Side of the Protestant Ethic: A Comparative Analysis of Welfare Reform." *Sociological Theory* 23 (1): 1–24.

Hunton, Alphaeus w. (1970). "W.E.B. Du Bois: the meaning of his life." In John Henrik Clarke et al (Eds.), *Black Titan: W.E.B. Du Bois* (pp. 131–137). Boston: Beacon Press.

Inkeles, Alex (1959). "Personality and Social Structure." In Robert K. Merton, Leonard Broom, and Leonard S. Cottrell, Jr. (eds.), *Sociology Today* (pp. 249–276). New York: Basic Books.

Inkeles, Alex (1960). "Industrial man: The Relation of Status, Experience, and Value." *American Journal of Sociology* 66: 1–31.

Inkeles, Alex (1969). "Making Men Modern: On the causes and consequences of individual change in six developing countries." *American Journal of Sociology* 75: 208–225.

Jameson, Fredric and Masao Miyoshi (ed.). (1998). *The Cultures of Globalization*. Durham: Duke University Press.

Jones, G.S. (1971). *Outcast London: A Study in the Relationship Between Classes in Victorian Society*. Oxford: Clarendon Press.

Jordan, Winthrop D. (1972). "Modern Tensions and the Origins of American Slavery." In Donald Noel (Ed.), *The Origins of American Slavery and Racism* (pp. 81–94). Ohio: Charles E. Merrill Publishing Co.

Kardiner, Abram and Lionel Ovesey (1962 [1951]. *The Mark of Oppression:Explorations in the Personality of the American Negro*. Meridian Ed.

Karenga, Maulana (1993). *Introduction to Black Studies*. California: The University of Sankore Press.

Kellner, Douglas (2002). "Theorizing Globalization." *Sociological Theory*, 20:3, 285–305.

Kneller, George F. (1964). *Introduction to the Philosophy of Education*. New York: John Wiley & Sons, Inc.

Kuhn, Thomas S. (1996). *The Structure of Scientific Revolutions* (Third Edition). Chicago: The University of Chicago Press.
Laclau, Ernesto and Chantal Mouffe (1985). *Hegemony & Socialist Strategy: Towards a Radical Democratic Politics*. New York and London: Verso.
Lester, Julius (ed.) (1971). *The Seventh Son: The Thought and Writings of W.E.B. Du Bois (Volume I)*. New York: Random House.
Lester, Julius (ed.) (1971). *The Seventh Son: The Thought and Writings of W.E.B. Du Bois* (Volume II). New York: Random House.
Lewis, David Levering (1993). *W.E.B. Du Bois: Biography of a Race 1868–1919*. New York: Henry Holt and Company.
Levine, Lawrence W. (1977). *Black Culture and Black Consciousness: Afro-American Folk Thought from Slavery to Freedom*. New York: Oxford University Press.
Lévi-Strauss, Claude (1963). *Structural Anthropology* (Claire Jacobson and Brooke Schoepf, Trans.). New York: Basic Books.
Lincoln, Eric C. and Lawrence H. Mamiya (1990). *The Black Church in the African American Experience*. Durham and London: Duke University Press.
Luckmann, Thomas (Ed.) (1978). *Phenomenology and Sociology: Selected Readings*. New York: Penguin Books.
Lukács, Georg (1971). *History and Class Consciousness: Studies in Marxist Dialectics* (Rodney Livingstone, Trans.). Cambridge, Massachusetts: The MIT Press.
Lukács, Georg (2000). *A Defence of History and Class Consciousness: Tailism and the Dialectic* (Esther Leslie, Trans.). London and New York: Verso.
Luscombe, David (1997). *A History of Western Philosophy: Medieval Thought*. Oxford: Oxford University Press.
Lyman, Stanford M. (1997). *Postmodernism and a Sociology of the Absurd and Other Essays on the "Nouvelle Vague" in American Social Science*. Fayetteville: The University of Arkansas Press.
Lyman, Stanford M. and Arthur J. Vidich (1985). *American Sociology: Worldly Rejections of Religion and Their Directions*. New Haven and London: Yale University Press.
Lyman, Stanford M. (1972). *The Black American in Sociological Thought*. New York.
Mageo, Jeannette Marie (1998). *Theorizing Self in Samoa: Emotions, Genders, and Sexualities*. Ann Arbor: The University of Michigan Press.
Massey, D.S., and Denton, N.A. (1993). *American Apartheid: Segregation and the Making of the Underclass*. Cambridge, MA: Harvard University Press.
Marable, Manning (1986). *W.E.B. Du Bois: Black Radical Democrat*. Boston: Twayne Publishers.
Marcuse, Herbert (1964). *One-Dimensional Man*. Boston: Beacon Press.
Marcuse, Herbert (1974). *Eros and Civilization: A Philosophical Inquiry into Freud*. Boston: Beacon Press.
Marshall, Gordon (Ed.) (1998). *A Dictionary of Sociology* (Second edition). Oxford: Oxford University Press.
Marx, Karl and Friedrich Engels (1964). *The Communist Manifesto*. London, England: Penguin Books.

Marx, Karl (1992 [1867]). *Capital: A Critique of Political Economy* (Volume 1, Samuel Moore and Edward Aveling, Trans.). New York: International Publishers.
Marx, Karl (1998 [1845]). *The German Ideology*. New York: Prometheus Books.
Mason, Patrick L. (1996). "Race, Culture, and the Market." *Journal of Black Studies*, 26: 6, 782–808.
Mead, George Herbert (1978 [1910]). "What Social Objects Must Psychology Presuppose." In Thomas Luckmann (Ed.), *Phenomenology and Sociology: Selected Readings* (17–24). New York: Penguin Books.
Meier, August (1963). *Negro Thought in America, 1880–1915: Racial Ideologies in the Age of Booker T. Washington*. Ann Arbor: The University of Michigan Press.
Meier, August and Elliott M. Rudwick (1976 [1966]). *From Plantation to Ghetto; an Interpretive History of American Negroes*. New York: Hill and Wang.
Mocombe, Paul C. (2004). "Who Makes Race Matter in Post-Industrial Capitalist America?" *Race, Gender & Class* 11, 4: 30–47.
Moore, Jerry D. (1997). *Visions of Culture: An Introduction to Anthropological Theories and Theorists*. Walnut Creek, California: AltaMira Press.
Moynihan, Daniel P. (1965). *The Negro Family*. Washington, D.C.: Office of Planning and Research, US Department of Labor.
Murray, Charles (1984). *Losing Ground: American Social Policy 1950–1980*. New York: Basic Books.
Myrdal, Gunnar (1944). *An American Dilemma: The Negro Problem and Modern Democracy*. New York: Harper & Row Publishers.
Nash, Gary B. (1972). "Red, White and Black: The Origins of Racism in Colonial America." In Donald Noel (Ed.), *The Origins of American Slavery and Racism* (pp. 131–152). Ohio: Charles E. Merrill Publishing Co.
Nietzsche, Friedrich (1956). *The Birth of Tragedy* and *The Genealogy of Morals* (Francis Golffing, Trans.). New York: Anchor Books.
Nobles, Wade (1987). *African American Families: Issues, Ideas, and Insights*. Oakland: Black Family Institute.
Noel, Donald L. (Ed.) (1972). *The Origins of American Slavery and Racism*. Columbus, Ohio: Charles E. Merrill Publishing Co.
Noel, Donald L. (1972). "A Theory of the Origins of Ethnic Stratification." In Donald Noel (Ed.), *The Origins of American Slavery and Racism* (pp. 106–127). Ohio: Charles E. Merrill Publishing Co.
Noel, Donald L. (1972). "Slavery and the Rise of Racism." In Donald Noel (Ed.), *The Origins of American Slavery and Racism* (pp. 153–174). Ohio: Charles E. Merrill Publishing Co.
Obeyesekere, Gananath (1997 [1992*]*). *The Apotheosis of Captain Cook: European Mythmaking in the Pacific*. Hawaii: Bishop Museum Press.
Ortner, Sherry (1984). "Theory in Anthropology Since the Sixties," *Comparative Studies in Society and History* 26: 126–66.
Outlaw, Lucius (1996). "Conserve" Races?: In Defense of W.E.B. Du Bois." In Bernard W. Bell et al (Eds.), *W.E.B. Du Bois on Race and Culture: Philosophy, Politics, and Poetics* (pp. 15–38). New York and London: Routledge.
Parsons, Talcott (1951). *The Social System*. Glencoe, Illinois: Free Press.

Parsons, Talcott (1954). *Essays in Sociological Theory.* Glencoe, Illinois: Free Press.

Parsons, Talcott (1977). *Social Systems and the Evolutions of Action Theory.* New York: Free Press.

Patterson, Orlando (1982). *Slavery and Social Death: A Comparative Study.* Cambridge, Massachusetts: Harvard University Press.

Phillips, U.B. (1918). *American Negro Slavery: A survey of the Supply, Employment, and Control of Negro Labor as Determined by the Plantation Regime.* New York: D. Appleton and Company.

Phillips, U.B. (1963). *Life and Labor in the Old South.* Boston: Little Brown.

Polanyi, Karl (2001 [1944]). *The Great Transformation: The Political and Economic Origins of Our Time.* Boston: Beacon Press.

Psathas, George (1989). *Phenomenology and Sociology: Theory and Research.* Washington, D.C.: University Press of America.

Rampersad, Arnold (1976). *The Art and Imagination of W.E.B. Du Bois.* Cambridge, Massachusetts: Harvard University Press.

Rao, Hayagreeva et al (2005). "Border Crossing: Bricolage and the Erosion of Categorical Boundaries in French Gastronomy," *American Sociological Review* 70: 968–991.

Reed, Adolph L. (1997). *W.E.B. Du Bois and American Political Thought: Fabianism and the Color Line.* New York and Oxford: Oxford University Press.

Reyna, Stephen P. (1997). "Theory in Anthropology in the Nineties," *Cultural Dynamics* 9 (3): 325–350.

Roediger, David R. (1999). *The Wages of Whiteness: Race and the Making of the American Working Class.* London and New York: Verso.

Rose, Sonya O. (1997). "Class Formation and the Quintessential Worker." In John R. Hall (Ed.), *Reworking Class* (pp. 133–166). Ithaca and London: Cornell University Press.

Rosenau, Pauline Marie (1992). *Post-Modernism and the Social Sciences: Insights, Inroads, and Intrusions.* Princeton, New Jersey: Princeton University Press.

Rubin, Vera (Ed.) (1960). *Caribbean Studies: A Symposium.* Seattle: University of Washington Press.

Sahlins, Marshall (1995a). *How "Natives" Think: About Captain Cook, For Example.* Chicago: University of Chicago Press.

Sahlins, Marshall (1995b). *Historical Metaphors and Mythical Realities.* Ann Arbor: University of Michigan Press.

Sahlins, Marshall (1990). "The Political Economy of Grandeur in Hawaii from 1810 1830." In Emiko Ohnuki-Tierney (Ed.), *Culture through Time: Anthropological Approaches* (pp. 26–56). California: Stanford University Press.

Sahlins, Marshall (1989). "Captain Cook at Hawaii," *The Journal of the Polynesian Society* 98; 4: 371–423.

Sahlins, Marshall (1985). *Islands of History.* Chicago: University of Chicago Press.

Sahlins, Marshall (1982). "The Apotheosis of Captain Cook." In Michel Izard and Pierre Smith (Eds.), *Between Belief and Transgression* (pp. 73 102). Chicago: University of Chicago Press.

Sahlins, Marshall (1976). *Culture and Practical Reason*. Chicago, IL: University of Chicago Press.
Said, Edward (1979). *Orientalism*. New York: Vintage Books.
Sarup, Madan (1993). *An Introductory Guide to Post-Structuralism and Postmodernism* (second edition). Athens: The University of Georgia Press.
Saussure de, Ferdinand (1972 [1916]. *Course in General Linguistics*, Edited by Charles Bally et al. Illinois: Open Court.
Schutz, Alfred (1978). "Phenomenology and the Social Sciences." In Thomas Luckmann (Ed.), *Phenomenology and Sociology: Selected Readings* (pp. 119 141). New York: Penguin Books.
Schutz, Alfred (1978). " Some Structures of the Life-World." In Thomas Luckmann (Ed.), *Phenomenology and Sociology: Selected Readings* (pp. 257 274). New York: Penguin Books.
Schwalbe, Michael L. (1993). "Goffman Against Postmodernism: Emotion and the Reality of the Self." *Symbolic Interaction* 16(4): 333–350.
Searle, John R. (1997). *The Mystery of Consciousness*. New York: The New York Review of Books.
Sennett, Richard (1998). *The Corrosion of Character*. New York: W.W. Norton & Company.
Sklair, Leslie (1995). *Sociology of the Global System*. Baltimore: Westview Press.
Skorupski, John (1993). *A History of Western Philosophy: English-Language Philosophy 1750–1945*. Oxford: Oxford University Press.
Slemon, Stephen (1995). "The Scramble for Post-colonialism." In Bill Ashcroft et al (Eds.), *The Post-colonial Studies Reader* (pp. 45–52). London and New York: Routledge.
Smedley, Audrey (1999). *Race in North America: Origin and Evolution of a Worldview* (Second edition). Boulder, Colorado: Westview Press.
Smiley Group, Inc. (2006). *The Covenant with Black America*. Chicago: Third World Press.
Smith M.G. (1960). "The African Heritage in the Caribbean." In Vera Rubin (Ed.), *Caribbean Studies: A Symposium* (pp. 34–46). Seattle: University of Washington Press.
Solomon, Robert C. (1988). *A History of Western Philosophy: Continental Philosophy Since 1750, The Rise and Fall of the Self*. Oxford: Oxford University Press.
Sowell, Thomas (1975). *Race and Economics*. New York: David McKay.
Sowell, Thomas (1981). *Ethnic America*. New York: Basic Books.
Spivak, Chakravorty Gayatri (1994 [1988]). "Can the Subaltern Speak?" In Patrick Williams and Laura Chrisma (Eds.), *Colonial Discourse and Post-Colonial Theory A Reader* (pp. 66–111). New York: Columbia University Press.
Stack, Carol B. (1974). *All Our Kin: Strategies for Survival in a Black Community*. New York: Harper & Row Publishers.
Stampp, Kenneth (1967). *The Peculiar Institution*. New York: Alfred Knopf, Inc.
Staples, Robert (ed.) (1978). *The Black Family: Essays and Studies*. California: Wadsworth Publishing Company.
Stewart, David and Algis Mickunas (1990). *Exploring Phenomenology: A Guide to the Field and its Literature* (Second edition). Athens: Ohio University Press.

Strauss, Claudia and Naomi Quinn (1997). *A Cognitive Theory of Cultural Meaning*. United Kingdom: Cambridge University Press.

Stuckey, Sterling (1987). *Slave Culture: Nationalist Theory and the Foundations of Black America*. New York and Oxford: Oxford University Press.

Sturrock, John (ed.) (1979). *Structuralism and Since: From Lévi-Strauss to Derrida*. Oxford: Oxford University Press.

Sudarkasa, Niara (1980). "African and Afro-American Family Structure: A Comparison," The *Black Scholar*, 11: 37–60.

Sudarkasa, Niara (1981). "Interpreting the African Heritage in Afro-American Family Organization." In Harriette P. McAdoo (Ed.), *Black Families*. California: Sage Publications.

Sundquist, Eric J. (ed.) (1996). *The Oxford W.E.B. Du Bois Reader*. New York and Oxford: Oxford University Press.

Thomas, Nicholas (1982). "A Cultural Appropriation of History? Sahlins Among the Hawaiians," *Canberra Anthropology* 5; 1: 60–65.

Thompson, E.P. (1964). *The Making of the English Working Class*. New York: Pantheon Books.

Thompson, E.P. (1978). *The Poverty of Theory and Other Essays*. New York: Monthly Review Press.

Tulloch, Hugh (1999). *The Debate on the American Civil War Era*. Manchester: Manchester University Press.

Turner, Ralph H. (1976). "The Real Self: From Institution to Impulse." *American Journal of Sociology* 81: 989–1016.

Turner, Ralph H. (1988). "Personality in Society: Social Psychology's Contribution to Sociology." *Social Psychology Quarterly* 51; 1: 1–10.

Tussman, Joseph and Jacobus TenBroek (1949). "The Equal Protection of the Laws."*California Law Review* 37;3:341–381.

Wallerstein, Immanuel (1982). "The Rise and Future Demise of the World Capitalist System: Concepts for Comparative Analysis." In Hamza Alavi and Teodor Shanin (Eds.), *Introduction to the Sociology of "Developing Societies"* (pp. 29–53). New York: Monthly Review Press.

Ward, Glenn (1997). *Postmodernism*. London: Hodder & Stoughton Ltd.

Watkins, S. Craig (1998). *Representing: Hip-Hop Culture and the Production of Black Cinema*. Chicago: The University of Chicago Press.

Weber, Max (1958 [1904–1905]). *The Protestant Ethic and the Spirit of Capitalism* (Talcott Parsons, Trans.). New York: Charles Scribner's Sons.

West, Cornel (1993). *Race Matters*. New York: Vintage Books.

West, David (1996). *An Introduction to Continental Philosophy*. Cambridge: Polity Press.

Whipple, Mark (2005). "The Dewey-Lippmann Debate Today, Communication Distortions, Reflective Agency, and Participatory Democracy." *Sociological Theory*, 23 (2): 156–178.

Williams, Raymond (1977). *Marxism and Literature*. Oxford: Oxford University Press.

Wilson, Kirt H. (1999). "Towards a Discursive Theory of Racial Identity: The Souls of Black Folk as a Response to Nineteenth-Century Biological Determinism." *Western Journal of Communication*, 63 (2): 193–215.
Wilson, William J. (1978). *The Declining Significance of Race: Blacks and Changing American Institutions*. Chicago and London: The University of Chicago Press.
Wilson, William J. (1987). *The Truly Disadvantaged*. Chicago and London: University of Chicago Press.
Winant, Howard (2001). *The World is a Ghetto: Race and Democracy since World War II*. New York: Basic Books.
Wittgenstein, Ludwig (2001 [1953]). *Philosophical Investigations* (G.E.M. Anscombe Trans.). Malden, Massachusetts: Blackwell Publishers Ltd.
Wright, Kai (editor) (2001). *The African-American Archive: The History of the Black Experience in Documents*. New York: Black Dog & Leventhal Publishers.
Woodson, Carter G. (1969 [1933]). *The Mis-Education of the Negro*. Washington: Associated Publishers Inc.
Young, Iris Marion (1994). "Gender as Seriality: Thinking about Women as a Social Collective," *Signs* 19: 713–738.
Zamir, Shamoon (1995). *Dark Voices: W.E.B. Du Bois and American Thought, 1888–1903*. Chicago & London: The University of Chicago Press.
Zeitlin, Irving M. (1990). *Ideology and the development of sociological theory* (4th ed.). Englewood Cliffs, New Jersey: Prentice-Hall.

Index

Adorno, Theodore, 99, 110, 111, 113
Allen, Ernest Jr., 55, 113
Allen, Richard L., 54–55, 113
Althusser, Louis, 99, 113
Appiah, Anthony, 57, 58, 113
Audacity of Hope: Thoughts on Reclaiming the American Dream (Obama), 84, 93

Baker, Houston, 55, 114
Balibar, Etinenne, 12
being-in-the-world: African forms of, 18, 20, 26, 88; assessment and reproduction of, 93; communicative action and, 25; double conciousness and, 39; purposive rationality and, 27; sanctioned conduct and, 22–23; social psychological nature of, 95; sociohistorical constructs and, 99
Bell, Bernard W., 54, 55, 114
Bhabha, Homi, 100, 102, 104, 105, 114
biological determinism, 3, 27, 57, 60, 65
black nationalism, 23
Black Panthers, 92
black practical consciousness: adaptive-vitality approach to, 64, 66–69, 76; capitalism and, 15; Du Bois on, 34; dualism and, 43; initial practical consciousness, 42; liberal black Protestant heterosexual bourgeois male and, 4, 14, 88; moral consciousness and, 96–97; Obama presidency and, 92, 98; pathological-pathogenic approach to, 64–67, 69, 71n4, 76, 88; purposive rationality and, 12, 24; race and class antinomy, 26; slavery and, 17–20, 88
black protest, 21–22, 109
black underclass: class identity, 73; creation of, 61, 83; double consciousness and, 87, 89; hip-hop culture, 61, 82, 91; Obama and, 61, 77, 84, 90–91, 95; predestination and, 52; social isolation, 32, 37, 94
Blassingame, John, 22, 114
Boxill, Bernard, 58, 115
Bruce, Dickinson D., 54, 71n5, 115

capitalism, 7-8, 11–15, 96, 101–3
Castro, Fidel, 104
class and race dialectic, 3, 14, 17
class identity, 10, 73, 87, 89
class racism, 47, 50, 68–69, 90
class-color-caste system, 23–24, 82
communicative action, 13, 17, 25, 27
communism, 51, 85, 90, 108

The Concept of Self: A Study of Black Identity and Self-Esteem (Allen), 54–55
consciousness formation, 43–44, 64, 99–100
"The Conservation of Races" (Du Bois), 56–57
The Covenant with Black America (Smiley), 93
Cuba, 105–6, 110
culture, structure of bourgeois, *11*

Delany, Martin, 23
domination, manifold forms of, 99
double consciousness construct: basis for, 57; Bell on, 54; bicultural reading of, 95; Bruce on, 54, 71n5; contemporary notions of, 53–59; deconstruction of, 40–42, 50, 59, 69, 71n5, 90; Lewis on, 54; origin of, 26; reinterpretation of, 89–90; validity of, 43, 55. *See also* Du Bois, W.E.B.
Dreams from My Father (Obama), 74, 76, 78–79
Du Bois, W.E.B.: ambivalence of, 38–42, 46–48, 50–51, 59, 63, 108; Americanism of, 36–38; biographical details of, 33–34; Boxill on, 58; class racism of, 47, 50, 68–69; communist pan-Africanism, 85, 90, 108; "The Conservation of Races," 56–57; development of his consciousness, 43–48; double consciousness and, 2–3, 26, 39–40, 43; at Fisk University, 36, 38, 44–45, 46; liberal black bourgeois Protestantism and, 2, 28, 63, 85; "A Negro Nation within a Nation," 51; Obama compared to, 63–64, 69, 76–77, 80–82, 84, 90–91; "Of Our Spiritual Strivings," 38; Outlaw on, 58; Protestant ethic and, 34–35, 48, 60; on racial equality, 49–50, 56–58; Rampersad on, 55; *The Souls of Black Folks*, 2, 28, 37, 39, 53, 55–57, 64, 93, 108; view of ordinary black people, 33–37; West on, 33–34; works of, 116

Elkins, Stanley, 22, 29n7, 65, 116

Fanon, Frantz, 69, 117
Frazier, E. Franklin, 65, 71n4, 82, 117

Garnet, Henry Highland, 23, 26
Garvey, Marcus, 26, 40
Gilroy, Paul, 55, 118
Glazer, Nathan, 65, 118
Gooding-Williams, Robert, 58, 118
Gramsci, Antonio, 48, 118

Habermas, Jürgen, 9, 10, 13, 17
Harding, Vincent D., 21, 118
heterogeneity (Bhabha and Spivak debate), 100–101
hip-hop culture, 61, 83, 91, 94
Hoover, J. Edgar, 92
Hybridity: black culture and, 64; identity and, 99, 104, 106, 109, 111; notion of (Bhabha), 97, 100, 102, 104; postcolonial, 100, 107

identity-in-differential, 47, 66, 104, 110, 112n1
ideological state apparatuses, 6–7, 43, 102–3
"Ideology and Ideological State Apparatuses" (Althusser), 99
integrationist movement, 92–95
"iron cage" thesis (Weber), 6, 13, 17, 29n3
Islamic fundamentalist movements, 105–7, 111–12

Jackson, Jesse, 77

Karenga, Maulana, 15–16, 64–65

Lester, Julius, 36, 120
Lewis, David Levering, 54, 120

liberal black Protestant heterosexual bourgeois male: ambivalence in, 26–28, 53, 69, 87; black practical consciousness and, 4, 88; double conciousness and, 59, 87; Du Bois and, 28, 63, 85; effect of, 91–93; hybridity and, 99; Obama and, 2, 62; purposive rationality of, 87

Marable, Manning, 55, 120
Marx, Karl, 104, 121
Meier, August, 54, 121
moral consciousness, 96–97
Moynihan, Daniel Patrick, 65, 121
Myrdal, Gunnar, 65, 121

Nation of Islam, 110
"Negative Dialectics" (Frankfurt school), 109–10
"A Negro Nation within a Nation" (Du Bois), 51
Negro Thought in America (Meier), 54

Obama, President Barack: ambivalence of, 2, 28, 70, 84, 95; *Audacity of Hope: Thoughts on Reclaiming the American Dream*, 84; biographical details of, 74–75, 78; black underclass and, 61, 77, 84, 90–91, 95; double consciousness and, 53, 63–65, 73, 75–77, 80–81, 83; *Dreams from My Father*, 74, 76, 78–79; Du Bois compared to, 63–64, 69, 76–77, 80–82, 84, 90–91; on faith, 78–80; hybridity and, 107, 109; liberal bourgeois Protestantism and, 1, 51, 60–61, 70, 73, 77, 80–85; meaning of his presidency, 98; Protestant ethic and, 6, 79, 82; racial identity of, 75–79
one drop rule, 77
"Of Our Spiritual Strivings" (Du Bois), 38, 56, 58–59
Outlaw, Lucius, 58, 121

The Philadelphia Negro (Du Bois), 26
predestination: American social formation and, 15–17, 24–25; black underclass and, 52; capitalism and, 8, 10, 16, 96; class identity, 10–11; Protestant ethic and, 6, 18; slavery, 20–22, 24, 25
Prosser, Gabriel, 23
Protestant ethic: American social formation and, 15; capitalism and, 11–13; Du Bois and, 6, 60; internal contradiction of, 12; Obama and, 6, 82; predestination and, 6, 18; purposive rationality, 7, 9, 44; slavery and, 22–23; Weber on, 6
The Protestant Ethic and the Spirit of Capitalism (Weber), 5, 6
Protestantism: capitalism and, 7-8; of Obama, 79–80; principles of liberal black bourgeois Protestantism, 59–60; radicalism and, 11; slavery and, 16–18
purposive rationality: acculturation and, 23, 24, 31n19; being-in-the-world and, 27; black practical consciousness, 12, 24; capital accumulation and, 10–13, 16, 102; consciousness formation and, 99–100; double consciousness and, 4, 40, 53, 87; ideological state apparatuses and, 103; institutionalized laws and practices, 17, 98; of liberal black Protestant heterosexual bourgeois male, 87; Obama and, 61; Protestant ethic and, 7, 9, 44; of white Protestant bourgeois heterosexual male, 6, 13–14, 99

race and racial worldviews, commodification of, 51, 53, 61, 82–83, 94
racism, 16, 29-30n12, 72, 80, 90. *See also* class racism
radicalism, 11

Rampersad, Arnold, 55, 122
Reed, Adolph, 26–27, 122
rule of forms, 111

secular modernity, 105
self-conscious manhood, 27, 46–47, 59, 76–77, 91
The Slave Community (Blassingame), 22
slavery: acculturation for survival, 22–24; American social formation and, 14–16; black practical consciousness and, 17–20, 88; black resistance to, 21–22; Christian beatitudes and, 22, 30n16; class-color-caste system, 23–24; Karenga on, 15–16; laws and judicial rulings concerning, 20–21, 25; predestination and, 20–22, 24; Protestantism and, 16–18; purposive rationality and, 23, 31n19; rationalization of, 16, 29n12; slave and free Negro population growth (1790-1860), *20*; slave personality explanation, 19
Social Darwinism, 47
social integration phenomenon, 106–7
social practices, regulation of, 14, 42
social psychological identity, 24
socialization, 43–44
sociohistorical processes and black consciousness, 64–65
The Souls of Black Folks (Du Bois), 2, 28, 37, 39, 53, 55–57, 64, 93, 108

Sowell, Thomas, 94, 123
Spivak, Gayatri Chakravorty, 100, 102–3, 123
Steele, Shelby, 70, 74, 86n7, 94
"Strivings of the Negro People" (Du Bois), 56
Sundquist, Eric J., 55, 124

Talented Tenth, 47, 48, 51
Trinity United Church of Christ, 78–80
Turner, Nat, 23
two theoretical consciousnesses theory (Gramsci), 48

Vesey, Denmark, 23

Walker, David, 23
Washington, Booker T., 23, 26, 40
"W.E.B. Du Bois and the Idea of Double Consciousness" (Bruce), 54
Weber, Max, 6–8, 13, 29n3. *See also* "iron cage" thesis (Weber)
West, Cornel, 33–34, 124
white nationalism, 25
white Protestant heterosexual bourgeois male: capitalistic social relations, 101–2; establishing society, 98, 101; ideological state apparatuses and, 102–3; purposive rationality of, 6, 13–14, 99; radicalism and, 11
Wilson, Kirt H., 56, 58, 125
Wright, Jeremiah Jr., 75, 77, 79, 85n5